KIDS STiLL HAViNG KIDS

TALKING ABOUT TEEN PREGNANCY

Revised Edition

BY JANET BODE
ART BY STAN MACK AND IDA MARX BLUE SPRUCE

FRANKLIN WATTS
DANBURY, CONNECTICUT
NEW YORK•LONDON•HONG KONG•SYDNEY

To Linda Feinberg Broessel

Copyright © 1999 by Janet Bode
Art copyright © 1999 by Stan Mack and Ida Blue Spruce Marx
All rights reserved.

Library of Congress Cataloging-in-Publication Data
Bode, Janet.
    Kids still having kids : talking about pregnancy /
by Janet Bode : art by Stan Mack and Ida Marx Blue Spruce.
—Rev. ed.
        p. cm.
    Includes bibliographical references and index.
    Summary : Presents interviews with teenage mothers and
provides information about adoption, parenting, abortion,
and foster care.
        ISBN 0-531-11588-7 (lib. bdg.)   0-531-15973-6 (pbk.)

    1. Teenagers—United States—Sexual behavior—Juvenile
literature. 2. Teenage pregnancy—United States—Juvenile literature.
3. Teenage parents—United States—Juvenile literature.
[1. Pregnancy. 2. Teenage parents. 3. Sex instruction for youth.]
I. Mack, Stan, ill. II. Blue Spruce, Ida Marx, ill. III. Title.
HQ27.B618 1998
306.7'0835-dc21   98-45477
                                                                    CIP
                                                                    AC

Printed in the United States of America

CONTENTS

PART I

KIDS

TALKING ABOUT

SEX, ViRGiNITY AND WHY WOULD YOU WANT TO BE A PARENT?

"The World Is Not Perfect."

Teen pregnancy

For some of you it's the topic for a school research paper. A life skills teacher says, "Explore a teen-related social issue and then write about it." Teen pregnancy is what you decide to study.

For others, it's your life. You know the exact moment when sore breasts and a late period turn into the reality of a surprise pregnancy. Reactions range from panic to pride to "I'm out of here." At minimum, girls also hope for a boyfriend around to tell the news.

This book can serve as a starting point for all of you in the gathering of facts and feelings. Beyond the statistics you'll discover a collection of real-life stories about love and sex, pregnancy and making decisions. In their own way, in their own words, each teen and adult answers the question, how do you handle the possibility of being a parent?

Censored and Banned

Three times over the last two decades, I've tracked the issue of teen pregnancy and parenting, searching for the most recent surveys and studies, asking questions and recording answers of those most directly involved. The results can be found in my two books, *Kids Having Kids,* published in 1980, and *Kids Still Having Kids,* published in 1992. Both won awards and generated a lot of mail from readers.

These books have another distinction. In school districts around the country, they've been censored, banned and removed from library shelves. Other librarians have been instructed that they can't loan either of them unless students ask by name for the title.

The world is not perfect. I wish there weren't any such problems as unwanted pregnancy, sexual abuse or failed foster care. But there are, and not writing about them won't make them vanish. In fact, only by examining them can society hope to find solutions.

For that reason, you have in your hands a revised edition of those earlier books. I tried to locate the then-teenagers I interviewed eight years ago. "How are you doing now?" I wanted to know. With one exception—Emily, a birth mother—it proved impossible.

In the past to protect the privacy of the adolescents speaking on those pages, I changed their names and certain identifying details. In this edition, however, one group of East Coast students said I could include the name of their school: Wallkill Senior High School, Wallkill, New York, about 70 miles north of New York City.

Two other groups—students from Sam Yeto High School Young Mothers' Program, Fairfield, California, located between Oakland and Sacramento and Argo Community High School, Summit, Illinois, in the Chicago suburbs—went further. Instead of my interviewing them, they wrote their own real-life stories and best advice to you, the reader.

Parallel Universes

You don't have to read this book from start to finish. Check the contents page and see if any of the chapters speak to you.

Let's say you haven't had sex but are writing a paper. These stories, I hope, will serve as cautionary tales. The boxed information contain statistics you might find helpful. In a way, you live in a parallel universe to your peers who are sexually active and risk pregnancy.

But lives can and do change.

By force or by choice virgins have sex—and you, too, may wake up to discover you suddenly have a personal interest in this issue. Just as true, those of you who've been sexually active can decide to reclaim your virginity. Some call it secondary virginity, where you take control over your body and your emotions. Simply because you've had sex doesn't mean you can't change your mind and wait once more until later.

Still, for any pregnant or parenting adolescent, remember this: You are not alone. People will help you.

Start today to gather information and to ask for advice from those you trust and respect. You want to make wise choices about what to do.

And finally, *not* making a decision is making a decision. This book is only a place to start. For yourself and your future—take a next step.

FEWER TEENAGE MOTHERS? MAYBE
Don Terry, *The New York Times*, 5/5/98

EXPERTS point to several factors for the overall decline [in teen pregnancies], including abstinence education, wider distribution and better use of contraception, fear of AIDS and other sexually transmitted diseases, and church programs and other neighborhood outreach programs.

"Why Would You Want to Be a Parent?"

Wallkill Senior High School, Wallkill, New York
Four students talking during a lunch break

Kevin: In this school a lot of girls are pregnant. But no one here in this group is. No way.

Jonathan: You can see it coming. The problems are there before they get pregnant. Pregnancy just makes everything worse.

Lilly: What I see is that usually they're hanging with the wrong crowd. Sometimes they have an abortion. Remember Gwinneth did.

Kate: I always wonder, "Why would you want to be a parent so young? You have your whole life in front of you." When we find out someone we know is pregnant, we ask her 20 questions. "Who's the dad? How long have you been with him? Did you use protection? What are you going to do about it?"

Lilly: I want to scream, "What are you thinking? Why are you so happy?" Pregnant at 16, and they gloat! They don't know what they've gotten into.

Kevin: There are plenty of programs for them. They can have home tutoring. They can take the kid to school for day care and then go to special classes for themselves.

Kate: If one of us got pregnant, well, nobody's perfect, but it's certainly nothing we see as a role model.

Jonathan: We're stressed enough. Besides school, once we get drivers' licenses, we're the family's transportation. Our parents complain we're out too much, but then they want us to "pick up some milk and drive your brother to practice." Plus I work 35 hours a week at a local restaurant.

Lilly: Starting at 12, I've worked in my parents' business.

Kevin: I'm a camp counselor and mow lawns in the summer. I earn about $3,000.

Lilly: I'm still a virgin. I'm dating a few guys, but right now I don't want a relationship. Later when I do, I'll look for someone loyal with a good sense of humor.

Kate: Yeah, but it's nice if they have a good butt, are honest and, yes, looks are semi-important.

Jonathan: I just had my heart broken. We're still going to the prom, but we're going as friends. Three hundred dollars to go with a friend. Sometimes it was easier when I was little and still thought girls had cooties.

Kate: You should try to move on, Jonathan. While you treated her like a queen, she walked all over you. Of course, I find all the wrong men for myself.

Kevin: That's the bell. Gotta go.

"Never Have a Baby to Save a Relationship."

Sam Yeto High School, Fairfield, California
Four students in a Young Mothers' Program, excerpts from their essays

Morva Jimerson: Some grown women have the mind of a child. They don't know how to take care of themselves, let alone a baby. But some teens have the mind of a grown-up. People shouldn't automatically criticize teenagers for having babies too young.

La'Keisha Turner: Some teens come from troubled families and think a baby will help them escape. Some teens have a baby because their boyfriend wants them to. And some teens have a baby just because they have unsafe sex.

Shereā Gillman: Trust me, never have a baby to save a relationship. The couple may be better for about a year, but from there it goes downhill. You will wind up raising a child alone.

I'm not saying you can't have sex. Just use protection and don't have a child yet, unless you are absolutely sure you can support it alone. Both emotionally and financially.

No man comes with a guarantee he'll be there for you. Never ever depend solely on him.

Shantaye Belcher: There are teenagers that think it's cool to have kids, but I have two and it is not easy. For all teen mothers, myself included, it's time to face your limitations, be strong in what you believe and set goals.

I have a vision of what I want my kids to accomplish in their lifetime. Now I'm figuring out what I have to do to help them do that.

"A Virgin Wouldn't Understand."

Amber, 16 Years Old

My best girlfriend makes me crazy. She's smart except about guys. Every other month she comes to me and says she's afraid she's pregnant. I say, "Didn't you learn anything last time?"

She says, "I didn't think. We were so caught up in it."

She tells me she'd feel weird discussing birth control with her boyfriend. I say, "You're close enough to have sex. You're not close enough to talk with him about birth control?"

"You're a virgin," she says. "You wouldn't understand. It just doesn't feel the same if you use a condom."

"Maybe you trust your boyfriend. But you're the one who's going to get pregnant."

"Nothing's going to happen to me," she always answers.

"Everyone's Having Sex but Me."

Lorenzo, 18 Years Old

There's a lot of pressure to have sex. And there's a lot of curiosity.

It's hard to have self-control. So some teenagers rush. They don't think that sex is more than sex. To me, it's a bonding between two people. It's intimate. It's about making a commitment.

I'm 18 and I haven't had sex. I'm sure guys hit 16, 17, 18, and they say, "Oh, I stopped being a virgin when I was 15."

They exaggerate so they won't feel out of place. They think, "Everyone's having sex but me." Sometimes I feel that way.

I have a group of friends and they're all having sex. Fathers tell sons, "Have sex, enjoy yourself." They think it's the manly thing to do.

A couple of months ago, my friends, like, found someone for me to have sex with. I knew, though, that I had an expression on my face. They guessed it would be my first time. They laughed and said, "You're a virgin!" I didn't know whether to hide it or fake it.

I thought of my mother. She says if a guy has sex with a girl and she gets pregnant, she goes through a lot. I would, too. How can I take the chance of having a child when I'm not even settled myself?

"I'm Facing the Question Whether to Have Sex."

Winona, 16 Years Old

A close friend of mine, the girl next door, has a two-year-old. Six months into her pregnancy, she decided to surprise me with the news. To this day it's hard for me to comprehend this happened to someone so much like me.

What scares me most is her family has been seriously disrupted by this whole situation. I don't understand why she kept her baby. She's still carefree, still living off her parents. She treats him like a little brother. She doesn't show she made any kind of mistake at all.

Now I'm facing the question whether to have sex. All I can think about is my neighbor's baby—with no dad and an airhead mom who was in a rush to grow up.

NEARLY 3,000 TEENAGERS AGE 13 TO 19 HAVE DEVELOPED AIDS

AIDS IS CAUSED by the human immunodeficiency virus (HIV). In most cases the virus is transmitted when you have unprotected sex with someone who is infected or when you share nonsterile needles to shoot drugs.

Since the epidemic started, nearly 3,000 teenagers age 13 to 19 have developed AIDS, as have 22,000 people age 20 to 24. It's estimated for every known case of AIDS, ten more people are infected with HIV. That means about a quarter of a million people between 13 and 24 may now be HIV-positive.

COMPLETE PROTECTION

FOR COMPLETE protection against HIV and AIDS, don't have sex and don't share hypodermic needles.

That advice aside, if you have sex, become pregnant and are infected with HIV or have AIDS, think about this. Studies show that 13 to 30 percent of babies born to HIV positive mothers end up with the virus, too.

Ask yourself these questions: Have I taken any medication that could damage the fetus? If I get sick or die, who will care for the baby? If the baby gets sick or dies, can I cope?

Jan Stollenwerk, School Nurse

San Diego, California

A student came to my office, sat down and said, "I think I'm pregnant."

"Oh, really?" I said, as we checked the calendar to see when she had her last period. "Do you have sex often?"

"No, this was my first time."

"When?"

"Saturday night."

This was Monday morning. I said, "Well, according to your menstrual cycle, I don't think you're pregnant right now. But you know what? That egg is just sitting there ready to pop out of the ovary. And that sperm is just sitting in the fallopian tube waiting for it. You might not be pregnant now, but it can happen any minute."

"Any minute? Oh, my gosh."

"Did you use protection—birth control?"

"Yes," she said, "but it fell off."

That means they didn't use anything.

"Does your boyfriend love you?" I said.

"Oh, yes."

"If you were out in the parking lot together and some guy came up and hit you, would he protect you?"

"Oh, yes. He'd punch his lights out."

"Why?"

"Why? He doesn't want me to get hurt."

I said, "Tell me. Did your boyfriend have a good time Saturday night?"

"Yes."

"Did you have a good time?"

"It was okay."

"Is your boyfriend out in the lunch court now?"

"Yes."

"Is he having a good time?"

"I guess so."

"Are you having a good time right now?"

"No."

"Are you going to have a good time tomorrow? What about for the next two weeks until your period comes? Are you going to have a good time?"

"No. I'm going to be worried about whether I'm pregnant."

"So you're worrying and hurting. Isn't that hurting you?"

"Yes."

I said, "Isn't this the same thing? Why doesn't your boyfriend take precaution and protection to keep you from all this pain you're going through? If he would protect you from a stranger hitting you, wouldn't he also want to protect you from this fear of pregnancy?"

"Well, yes, he would."

"Exactly. You want to be protected. He should be the protector."

UNDER REPORTING FOUND ON MALE TEENAGER SEX

Amy Harmon, The New York Times, 5/8/98

MALE teenagers engage in risky behavior associated with HIV infection more than previously thought. Among the males ages 15 to 19 surveyed nationally, 5.5 percent report some type of male-male sex; 2.8 percent report sex with an intravenous drug user; and 10.8 percent report they were "always" or "often" drunk or high when they had heterosexual sex.

"I Refuse to
Stop Loving Him."

Sydney, 17 Years Old

I'm not pregnant, but, you know, I've been in that place where I thought I was. Being raised in a Christian home, it was hard to confront my parents about having sex. But I did.

My parents said, "It's your choice. But if you don't quit, you and that boyfriend of yours have to come tell us together. And you can be sure our reaction is not the one you want."

I've been with this guy a very long time. For my parents' sake, I quit having sex for a while, but then I started again, which forced me to lie to my family.

Finally, I was sick of hiding. I came clean. Now that was a fight. They were yelling, "You don't have the means to provide for yourselves, let alone any possible baby."

"Even if you're right," I yelled back, "I'm only two weeks away from graduating. I refuse to stop loving him!" I didn't add "and I want to live with him." How would you start that conversation?

What would you do in my situation?

TEEN SEXUAL ABUSE

The Brown University Child & Adolescent Behavior Letter, May 1998 (University of Southern California News)

GIRLS who were sexually abused as children are far more likely both to practice risky sexual behavior and to become pregnant as adolescents, according to a study from the National Institute of Mental Health.

The study's investigators report that not only were sexually abused girls more likely to have babies, they also were more likely to be sexually active at a younger age and had more children than did girls who had not been abused. The findings were not affected by socioeconomic status.

PART II

KIDS
TALKING ABOUT
PREGNANCY,
FAiLED BiRTH CONTROL,
ROACHES AND CHOiCES

"My Birth Control Failed."

Marisol, 17 Years Old

I'm the oldest.

My mom had me when she was 17. I didn't know my real dad until I was 10. Partly, I was raised by my sisters' and brothers' dad. I considered him my father. My real dad is nothing special.

My mom's a single parent now. She works the graveyard shift. It's hard financially. She has to get us stuff at the secondhand store. Still, I'm happy with the way she's bringing us up.

One thing I like is she's open about sex. She tells me and my sisters and brothers that it's normal. Every human being gets sexual feelings with the right person at certain times.

And even if it isn't the right person, if we feel we want to experiment—to have intercourse—come to her first. She'd be upset, but that's just being a parent. We should know there are birth-control precautions to take.

Gorgeous

I started seeing my boyfriend, Nicholas, three years ago. From the moment we met, I'm thinking, he's gorgeous. I'm afraid he thinks I'm just a friend. I put a letter in his car telling him I like him.

He calls me that same day.

My heart starts beating. Fast. I'm embarrassed. "I never thought you'd notice me," I say. He's mellow. He likes country music, caving, hiking where there're trees.

Back then, I'm more like this wild person. Not partying, but I'm up to everything—all the new fads. I'm going to school and working 40 hours a week at Senn's Boutique. I have money.

He says, "I never expected you to like someone like me. I wanted to ask you out, but I didn't know how."

My friends think we're a really cute couple. They tease, "Oh, let us borrow Nick. He's so sexy."

At first, my mom and him don't hit it off. She gives him the cold shoulder. She doesn't want him to take away her oldest daughter. Next she's trying to like him, but he's Anglo, white. She's Mexican.

My grandmother isn't happy, either. She feels I'm Mexican—I should marry a Mexican guy.

After seeing Nicholas for a while, I know I have these sexual feelings about him. He's dropping me off at my house after a date. I say to him, "Let's sit on the porch and talk. I have something to ask you."

He keeps looking at my face, going, "What?"

I go, "Nothing. I don't know how to tell you."

"Go ahead."

"I'm embarrassed."

It takes me a half hour to say I have sexual feelings for him. And I don't know if he has the same feelings for me. He say he does, but he doesn't want to pressure me.

"You're not," I say. "I'm the one who brought up the subject. If it's okay, I'll talk to my mom about getting birth control." The next day I don't plan a speech— I just tell my mom I have to talk to her.

"About what?" she says.

"About me and Nicholas."

I think she has an idea what I'm going to say, but she wants me to come out and say it.

"I'm having sexual feelings for him, and I want to get birth control."

"Are you sure?" she says.

"Yeah."

"Well, I guess we'll make a doctor's appointment. I want you to know, though, this is hard for me."

A Guy Doctor?

Let me tell you, for me, it's hard to go to a GYN doctor for the first time. I think it will be no big deal. Go in. Get a prescription for birth control pills. That's it.

Wrong.

My mom keeps telling me, "You're going to have a pap smear."

"What's that?"

She says, "It's a test for cervical cancer. The cervix is at the end of your uterus. You go in the examining room, put your feet up on these stirrup things. The doctor sticks something in you that looks like a duck's beak. He'll stick his fingers in you to check your ovaries and stuff."

"No way," I go.

"If you want to be on birth control, yes, he is."

Then she tells me I have to feel my boobs to make sure I don't have lumps, possible breast cancer.

"It's going to be a guy doctor?" I say. And in comes this man. I'm so embarrassed.

My mom stays in the room with me. I want her to. I'm only 16.

After the exam, the doctor gives me a real pretty case with a butterfly on it that has pills inside. He tells me to take a pill the Sunday after I start my period. Then take it every day for a month before I have intercourse.

"That's all?" I say.

"Yes, but you might want to use something else as a precaution not to get pregnant. The pill is about 96 percent to 99 percent effective. Remember, there's always that small percent that fail."

So I'm taking the pills, every day, at the same time. I'm not doing anything wrong. My period is still coming down. But I notice that my pants aren't fitting me anymore. My stomach's hurting. I'm nervous.

I go into my mom's room and tell her, "I don't know what's wrong with me." I show her my stomach.

"We'd better make a doctor's appointment."

The doctor tells me to lie down. He looks at my stomach. "You're definitely pregnant."

I go to the laboratory for a blood test. I'm 24 weeks pregnant. Not me! I am shocked! I'm that small percent.

Nicholas is excited. "I'm gonna be a daddy!" he says, and then he hugs me.

Bonnie Groh, Teen-Parent Director
Delta Schoolcraft Intermediate School District,
Escanaba, Michigan

Nine percent of teen mothers attempt suicide. That's about seven times the national rate for teenage girls who are not mothers. I worry about that.

Why It Happened

Let's say you didn't want to become pregnant. You even took the pill, one of the safest and most popular birth control methods. But maybe you weren't careful to take it every day about the same time.

Or you had the flu and threw up in the morning. You were on an antibiotic. You didn't know that meant the pill wasn't absorbed like it should be. You should have used two methods of protection, if you had sex.

If yours is a surprise pregnancy, you need to think about why it happened. You don't want to become pregnant again for the same reason.

Even when you're pregnant, you still have choices.

When I have teenage girls in conflict, I ask them, "What do you think are your choices?" Usually they bring up these options: keep the child, adoption, abortion or temporary foster care until they're ready for parenting. Some wonder, "do I or don't I want to get married?" Most, however, are choosing not to get married.

If you're pregnant, talk to an adult you trust—a parent, a favorite teacher, a counselor, a doctor you can count on to give you correct advice. Whether a pregnancy is planned or unplanned, making decisions about what to do is a lot to handle, especially on your own. The decisions you make should be part of a plan. Impulse decisions simply force you to deal with the consequences later. Start planning what to do about a pregnancy by answering these questions:

17 Questions

- How do I feel about the direction I'm going in life?
- What are my goals?
- If I have a child now, are those goals possible?
- Can I stick with my schooling?
- Is medical care easy to get and affordable?
- If my eating habits aren't the best, am I willing to change them and eat well during and after the pregnancy?

- Is the father around? Is he supportive? Will he be supportive five or 10 years from now?
- Do the two of us share the same values and feelings about the importance of the family and how to take care of and raise a child?
- Can one or both of us get a decent job so we won't have to live in poverty?
- Am I compulsive about spending or am I good at stretching the dollar? Can I cover my expenses for food, clothing, and rent—plus for a child?
- Will my family be there as part of my support system?
- Will they still help out once the child is a toddler—more adventuresome and harder to raise?
- Is affordable day care available? Will I have to arrange transportation in order to get there? Do they take infants, as well as toddlers and above?
- Do I like caring for a baby? A toddler? A teenager?
- How do I handle my anger and frustration? Would I ever take out my emotions on a child?
- Am I willing to give up lots of my freedom and my social life to take on the responsibility of raising a child—for at least the next 18 years?
- Can I give a child the future I'd want for him or her?

Painful

Making decisions about a pregnancy can be painful. It's painful to raise a child. It's painful to relinquish a child for adoption. It's painful to have an abortion. But this doesn't mean you should put off these decisions.

Hoping you aren't pregnant won't make it go away.

SEXUALLY TRANSMITTED DISEASES (STDS)

Facts in Brief, The Alan Guttmacher Institute, 7/96

EVERY YEAR 3 million teens—about 1 in 4 sexually experienced teens—acquire an STD. In a single act of unprotected sex with an infected partner, a teen female has a 1 percent risk of acquiring HIV, a 30 percent risk of getting genital herpes and a 50 percent chance of contracting gonorrhea.

Chlamydia is more common among teens than among older people. In some settings, 10–29 percent of sexually active teenage women and 10 percent of teenage men tested for STDs have chlamydia.

Teens have higher rates of gonorrhea than do those sexually active aged 20–44. In some studies, up to 15 percent of sexually active teen females have been found to be infected with human papillomavirus (HPV), many with a strain linked to cervical cancer.

Teen females have a higher hospitalization rate than older women for acute pelvic inflammatory disease (PID), which is most often caused by untreated gonorrhea or chlamydia. PID can lead to infertility and ectopic pregnancy.

"Girls Came out Like Roaches."

Written by
Aurelio Estrada, 17 Years Old
Argo Community High School, Summit, Illinois

Right after grammar school my attitude took a 180° turn for the worst. For me, life was The Street. Fifty dollars got me going. With that I bought an ounce of weed. I'd sell it and make more than a hundred. Invest that again—I kept doubling my profits. Once I had the money, girls came out like roaches.

Bear RIP

I ain't gonna lie and say I hated my life. I loved it. Money, I learned, gets you anything you want. But there were the drawbacks, like, my parents and me were always arguing. They wanted me to go to school and stop hanging with the wrong crowd. My kind of life could bring me down, they'd always say. I didn't want to listen.

My mom was disappointed. No matter what, though, she loved me. She waited up to make sure I got home safe.

My dad was different. He'd go to the 'hood to look for me. Once I saw him when I was with my boys Rocket and Bear RIP. Bear passed away less than a year ago.

My dad went up to Bear and said, "How old are you?"

Bear didn't know that was my dad, so he got mad and asked him back, "How old are you?"

"That's Aurelio's dad," Rocket told him. He apologized and tried to shake his hand. My dad just looked at him and came toward me, saying, "I want you home." I stayed on the street.

Blunts and Bums

Sometimes I'd go to school. But before we went inside, guys and girls, too, we'd smoke a blunt or send a bum to buy us a bottle of vodka. We'd sit in first period blasted. I'd talk to my girl, Isela, but by third period I was asleep. I'd leave at 12:30, when some seniors left to go to work.

By the summer before my junior year, I didn't hesitate to do anything. I was getting arrested for curfew, mob action, aggravated battery, possession of a concealed weapon. The police would throw me in the can, and in a little bit, I'd get out.

I didn't care. It was back to partying, busting out, kickin' back, looking for some flakes or just waiting for them to pass by.

Nothing ever really happened to me, but I was seeing friends die. I lost eight of my boys in two years. For each one of *us* to go down, I thought six of *them* should fall. And in a few cases, that did happen.

I had no remorse. To me they were nobodies. What mattered was making sure my boys' memories didn't leave just because they were Resting in Peace (RIP).

The First Shot

I remember the first time I got shot at. I wasn't even gangbangin'. I was a fifth-grader walking home from school. Some white boy D's from the projects started shooting at some Kings. Even though I was small, I reacted the right way. I ducked behind a car until they stopped. Things like that happened so much that my parents decided we had to move to a quiet neighborhood. And it was until we all grew up and started hanging with the older kids.

A Good Father

As much as I say I loved my life, when my girlfriend told me she was pregnant, I kind of seen that it was no real life. It wasn't what I wanted my baby to be raised up in. I wanted something better. I knew I had to try to change myself.

Her parents did know—well, her mom knew—all about me. My old dean called them over to school to tell them everything she knew, which was a lot. The Chicago police helped her out with more information.

Still even if I was bad and looked bad, I always talked to my girl's parents with respect. In fact I talked to most adults with respect. My parents knew I did that, too, so they tried to control their anger at me.

They would never turn their backs on me or any grandchild. I promised my girlfriend I'd calm down and I did. I was doing good. I was looking to the future.

Then she lost the baby.

I don't know what happened, but I knew I wasn't gonna be a father. I would have no responsibilities. I quit my office job, where I answered phones, ran errands, filed and entered data on the computer. For a while I went back to doing what I always did, which was nothing. But then I realized, I'm getting older. I do want to change.

Life is more than the street.

Today I'm trying to get myself together. I'm willing to do whatever I have to keep myself studying and graduate. I want to go into the navy or find a way to become an FBI or ATF agent. That's what I want to be. I want to be a cop, but not one of those in uniform cops. I'm trying and, hopefully, I'll get to do it.

Then I'll be ready to be a good father.

David Berger, Chief, Department of Pediatrics
Gouverneur Hospital
New York City, New York

Teenagers have more problem pregnancies than women in their 20s. More of your babies are premature and have low birth weights. Why?

You don't always go to a clinic early and often enough for what's called prenatal care. "Prenatal" means before the birth.

As soon as you think you might be pregnant, visit a clinic. You get commonsense counseling, testing and medical information. Your questions are answered. And in most locations, teenagers receive this care free.

How often you go to the clinic depends on your needs. If you're healthy and everything is okay, you see a health care worker a couple times during the first trimester—the first three months—and three or four times the second trimester. By the third trimester, you have to go more often, usually about every two weeks.

Pickles and Ice Cream

Let's say you're at the clinic. You've learned that a baby can be born with problems based on what you, the mother, are doing to yourself during the pregnancy. You know you shouldn't smoke, drink alcohol or do illegal drugs. But you don't know you should also watch what you eat.

You ask, "Why am I dying for pickles and ice cream in the middle of the night?" We tell you the truth. We have no earthly idea, but it happens. You're normal.

You say, "Since I'm eating for two, can I eat a lot more?" At most, you can eat 500 more calories a day. That's a second portion at dinner. You want to gain a total of 25 to 30 pounds.

You should try to limit an eat-and-run diet of McDonald's. Fast foods have little nutritional value, are often high in fat and salt content, low in iron and other minerals. Just being low in something like iron is tough on the fetus growing inside you. The baby's blood system is developing, and that takes iron. And you, the mother, may become iron deficient. By the time you notice tiredness, weakness or mental delays remembering things, you and the fetus could be in trouble.

At your prenatal checkups, we give you iron supplements, and you learn what's best to eat.

Duck-Walk and STDs

During a pregnancy, you go through physical changes. Your pelvic joints loosen, which means the way you walk changes—some call it a duck-walk. If you're brunette, you get a darkening around the face. You may experience swollen legs, feet and hands, water retention, backaches and frequent urination, among other things.

At the same time, you go through emotional changes. While each person has different reactions, as your body changes, your self-image changes. In prenatal care you talk about how you feel about these things.

You can also discuss how your relationships change with your family, friends and the father of your child. It's normal for you to have mood swings, to be excited, to be afraid. Every pregnant person goes through that, even women who want the baby more than anything.

Before the delivery we need to know if you have diabetes, high blood pressure or other such conditions.

We need to know, too, if you have any sexually transmitted diseases [STDs]—chlamydia, syphilis, gonorrhea, herpes.

And although we don't routinely test for HIV or AIDS, we do what's called a "risk assessment." We tell you your options and let you decide if you want to be tested.

Finally, together, we start planning for the delivery and, equally important, what happens after that big day. For yourself, for your child, it is much more dangerous and complicated if you don't come in until you are due. My best advice? Have regular pre- and postnatal visits.

"If I Could Change My Past, I Would."

Alison, 16 Years Old

"Are you a virgin?" Bobby asked me on our first date. We had skipped school and spent the whole day together. Right away I felt like I knew him forever.

"No," I said, wishing that wasn't the answer.

"Well, how come you didn't wait?" he said, 'cause he had.

"If I could change my past, I would. It's something you're going to have to live with."

We asked each other more questions. What his life and mine were like.

Bobby was beat a lot. His dad was an alcoholic. I told him I was sort of a party animal, into drinking. And I did try drugs. He said, "You don't need to get drunk or high. If I ever catch you, that's the end."

I told him my parents believed in the belt, too. I didn't. I was only allowed out once a weekend, Saturday until 11:00 P.M. even if I behaved. They were afraid of me getting pregnant. Bobby had a 23-year-old sister with two divorces, two kids, and no money. He didn't want that to happen to him.

Too Busy Crying

On prom night, a couple months after our first date, we took a back road home and talked about sex. "We're not going to do anything until we have protection," he said.

I'd never used anything before. I'd even had a close call where my period didn't come for three months. I didn't expect to hear that. Most guys are pushy. I'd never waited like this. It felt different.

Bobby even went with me to Planned Parenthood for the pills.

Three days later, my dad picked me up after my job. When I was in the bank cashing my check, he went through my purse. He found the pills. Well, he threw a fit.

"Would you rather have me not use anything?" I asked him.

"It's not right," he said. "I'm ashamed of you."

My ma told me it was hard to accept that I didn't go to her.

"I was scared," I said. "We never really talked about sex. I didn't want you to forbid me to see Bobby."

Bobby didn't come over for a while after that. Then he came over, but stayed outside and honked. Finally, I persuaded him to come in. He thought they'd hate him, thinking he'd forced me into doing something. But really, it was both of our choice.

My dad said, "You can only see Bobby once a weekend—here. We're doing this for your own good."

"You don't understand," I said. "I'm really hurting. You're taking away something that I really care about." Me and Bobby wanted to be alone.

They would yell. I wouldn't. I was too busy crying.

My parents figured if I didn't have the pills, I wouldn't have sex. They figured wrong.

I had a year's prescription. My dad had only taken one month's supply. I used them until I ran out. I never went back to get more. I didn't tell Bobby. There were a couple times I'd forgotten to take a pill. I thought we were careful enough.

Maybe two months later, though, I had signs. I was late. My breasts hurt bad. I had to go to the bathroom a lot.

What am I going to do? was my first thought.

I went to the health department to get a pregnancy test. It came back negative. I was confused. Maybe all those signs were nerves. I was upset. I took some pamphlets on teen pregnancy. I didn't know anything.

On New Year's, my ma asked, "Are you pregnant?"

"No," I told her, since my test had been negative. Two weeks later I took a home pregnancy test. Positive. I didn't know what happened with that first one. The doctor said, "Sometimes there's a mistake."

I was alone when I took it. I knew there was no reason to be sad. Bobby would always be there for me. When I told him, he was happy. He knew he had to take on the responsibility. And he was willing to do that. He'd get a job. We were both scared of telling our parents. We didn't want them to hate us. Finally, I told his ma. She told his dad.

"Well, look what a mess you got into now," his dad said to him. "Your ma and me were too young, too. We never had a good life. We never went to college. We didn't want that to happen to you."

Bobby told him not to worry. I was going to take a year off after I had the baby. Then I was going to sign up for college.

I first let my dad know over the phone. I reminded him that Ma was 19 when she had me. And my gramma was 17 when she had her first child. I could handle it.

An Icky Environment

I'm about six months pregnant now. As soon as I met Bobby, I started gaining weight. I went from a skinny 100 pounds to 120. What with being pregnant, now I weigh 146.

Bobby still loves me. He tells me that all the time. He's given me everything I've ever wanted—not just buying me things, either. He really shows me that he cares.

Like, I try to eat real good. I eat breakfast every morning, usually a bowl of cereal. A hot lunch at school. Then I eat supper. I like to have a snack, too, and Twinkies are my favorite.

Usually Bobby will buy me a can of fruit. But yesterday he knew I felt uncomfortable. He bought me a bunch of Twinkies and hid them in my locker. It was so cute.

I love spinach. Now I can't even look at it. I can't have salt, either. I can't have pop, because there's salt in it. My blood pressure is up. I've had swelling in my feet and legs. It's hard for me to bend over.

The doctor says, "You hold a lot of water in your body." He's afraid of toxemia. He never explains what that means. He just says it's when the baby is in an icky environment. If I get it, they have to do an emergency C-section. That's where they cut you open and take out the baby.

Last Sunday night, the baby didn't move. The next morning it still didn't move. I got scared. I went to the doctor's office, but he found the heartbeat. It was strong. He said, "Don't worry. Babies are like people. They have days when they like to be lazy."

All my family pats my belly and says, "Boy, you're getting big." It's brought me and my ma closer. My dad's more understanding, too.

I feel like I've grown up. I'm taking things more seriously. Every penny I get now goes toward the baby. I'm getting mostly used things, but it still adds up. We got a cradle. That was $50, brand-new. We got a crib, five dollars, used. We have to get a stroller, a car seat, a high chair. We need a ton of clothes, like sleepers and stuff.

But me and Bobby are not taking it fast. We're not getting married. We're getting engaged. He has a part-time job now that pays $100 a week. Once it's summer, he can work full-time. We don't know what kinds of problems we'll face. But we agree, if something happens, we'll talk it out.

It's funny. This started out about love and sex. Now that I'm pregnant, I never feel like having sex anymore. It hurts. Bobby's understanding.

You know, I'm happy about being pregnant and everything. My girlfriends are happy, too. They consider themselves aunties. They know that me and Bobby will never break up. Still...there were things that I wanted to do. I wish I would have waited.

BIRTH RATES FOR TEENAGERS DECLINED SHARPLY

Tamar Lewin, *The New York Times*, 5/1/98

EACH YEAR more than a million teenagers become pregnant. Of that total, there are 500,000 live births to those ages 15 to 19 and 11,000 to girls 14 and under. In addition, 400,000 receive abortions and 130,000 miscarry.

The level of teenage births was far higher in the 1950s and 1960s. But in those days, the vast majority of teenage mothers were married, while today, the vast majority are single.

Teenage birth rates vary greatly by state, with many Northern states like Vermont, New Hampshire, Minnesota, North Dakota, Maine and Massachusetts having less than half the rate of Southern and Western states like Alabama, Arizona, Georgia, Mississippi, New Mexico and Texas. Despite the declining rates, the United States still has by far the highest rate of teenage births of any industrialized nation.

Bill Cannon, Young Fathers Counselor
The Door,
New York City, New York

I work with young fathers. Generally when it's still a pregnancy, you want to be involved. What happens between then and when the baby arrives—that's a different story.

I try to help expectant fathers realize this pregnancy is a big thing. Your life changes. Just being told you're going to be a father produces anxiety. Inside you feel stress. Outside, though, you're, "Hey, it's cool. Let's swing with it."

If you're in this situation, and you come to me, I say, "Let's talk about what your life is like now." I try to get you to think about how you'd be if your girlfriend wasn't pregnant.

"What's happening at home?" I ask. "What kind of relationship do you have with your father? Are you in school? How are you doing? What are your plans for the future?"

Once you get a handle on that, you should think about exactly how your life will change if you become a father.

Minimum Wage at Burger King?

There's no storybook father, no storybook family relationship. You don't automatically end up with 3.2 kids in a home with a backyard and a dog. You have to look squarely at your life. How can you put things together to be the best father possible?

What comes up a lot is this: How can you understand what it is to be a father when you never really knew your own dad? Maybe you're in the same situation he was. And you definitely have some feelings about that.

You know what his absence has meant to you. You might not be able to talk about it, but the anger you feel translates into your not wanting your kids to grow up like that.

You should think, "What kind of father do I want to be?"

Maybe you say, "I'm going to be there for my kids. I'm going to do things with them. I'm going to talk to them when they have problems."

You've got this child on the way. You want to do the right thing. You've explored what your life is like. Now let's talk about what your options are. For starters, how are you going to support that child? You tell me you quit school. You've got to find a job, and you're thinking about dealing drugs.

Well, if you deal, there's a strong possibility you'll wind up either in jail or dead. If that happens, you take yourself away from the child you want to have a life with.

If you're sitting in my office, I tell you that.

What I hear is, "Okay, I won't deal drugs. But, man, come on, minimum wage at Burger King?!"

At this point, though, you don't have the skills to get a better-paying job. That's reality. If you want to be involved with your son or daughter, you have to work at minimum wage—for now.

This doesn't mean you have to do it for the rest of your life. Organizations like the one I work for can help you, or you can help yourself get back into school or take the GED. There is a future.

Maybe the idea of working for minimum wage makes you mad. But you made the decision to have this child, which means that it's no longer entirely about you. Now a major part of your time is spent preparing for your child to live in this world. You have to start accepting that you are responsible for that individual.

A Survival Mechanism

A good father begins now to look to the future. You do things that will ensure that the child will eat, grow and develop in as healthy a way as possible.

I won't put down a set standard. Each of you has to consider your own situation. A good father in many cases is someone who's doing the best he can. He's trying regardless of obstacles.

It's hard being a male in this society. You are raised and socialized to be screwed up in how to interact with the world around you, and particularly with your female partner.

And, generally, males feel that part of what defines manhood is fathering children. Just because you don't have a job, or you don't have a stable family support system, or the future is unclear, that will not necessarily keep you from fulfilling that aspect of your manhood.

In fact, if all those other things aren't in place, if you're feeling low self-esteem for all those reasons, you may look to fathering a child as the one thing that will establish your manhood.

I have a theory. I think that fathering children at a young age—particularly among so-called minorities—is a survival mechanism. Not only survival as an individual, but survival as a people.

On a certain level you know that things are not great for a lot of African-American people, for a lot of Latino people. I do believe that part of what's happening is a sense of realizing that these communities are in danger of being wiped out.

Driving Me Crazy

I often hear, "My f---ing girlfriend's driving me crazy!"

If the relationship with your girl doesn't work out, that happens. That does not mean right then and there you break off your relationship with your son or daughter. Instead, for however long you can, you should be involved in the development of your child.

PART III

KIDS TALKING ABOUT

ABORTiON, MiSCARRiAGE AND THE BEST-WORST SOLUTiON

Paula Wendt, Former Clinic Director
Meadowbrook Women's Clinic, Minneapolis, Minnesota

Most teenagers know that abortions are legal. They have been since 1973. But you don't know that the majority of states now have what's called either a parental consent law or a parental notice law. In both cases you first have to go to your parents and tell them you want to have an abortion.

If you don't want to tell one or both parents, there is a judicial bypass. You make an appointment to appear before a judge who, after hearing your situation, usually signs a petition saying you can have the abortion without a parent knowing.

As soon as you think you might be pregnant, confide in someone. Then you've got two heads working on it, instead of just one. You need somebody who's going to say to you, "We have to find out the facts right away."

Some of you say, "But I can't tell anyone I might be pregnant. I want an abortion."

Personally, I think this is the kind of life event that you need to share with others. And once you start sharing, you get a lot of support. Usually, you end up telling someone who's had an abortion or knows somebody who had an abortion.

I hear all the time, "I told my friend Mary I was pregnant and maybe going to have an abortion. Mary said, 'Well, I was never going to tell you this, but...'"

I'd like you to know that often parents are okay people to tell. Yes, you hear, "I'm hurt to learn this. I'm disappointed." But next you hear, "I love you. Your well-being is my priority. I want to help you."

I've also met parents who say to their daughter, "You tramp. Now that I know you're pregnant, you're never going to see that boy again!"

You can have an abortion without telling your parents. But you never forget that you did it. Do you want to have that secret until you're 25 or 30 and decide to share it with your mom?

What you might hear then is, "Didn't you love me enough to tell me?"

You answer, "That's exactly why I didn't tell you. I loved you so much."

Parents have a hard time with that. Then again, there are some parents who should never know. You know your parents better than any counselor. After discussing it with an adult you trust, you make the judgment whether to go to them.

Caught and Punished

If there's a chance you're pregnant, buy an at-home pregnancy test. For $10 or $15, you can test yourself when nobody's around. Then call a Planned Parenthood or a women's health clinic with a medical staff and go in for pregnancy testing and decision counseling.

You want to start thinking and talking about your options in a pregnancy. How do you see your future if you continue the pregnancy, parent the child, arrange for an adoption?

Only after those conversations do we talk about abortion. By this time, most of you say, "I always thought abortion was okay. I just never thought it would happen to me."

Some of you only had sex once, and now you're

pregnant. You feel caught and punished. It's hard to have to deal with all this. You feel you're being blamed for something you hardly did. Some of you ask, "If I have an abortion, will I go to hell?"

What I say is this: "I talk to a lot of women about that. Most say they feel God is forgiving. He understands that sometimes women need to do this."

Others say, "My parents will kill me if they find out I'm pregnant. But if I have an abortion, God will never forgive me."

"Then you must not have the abortion," I say. "To pay that kind of eternal, moral price is more than anybody should do."

Still others say, "I want to have the abortion, but I don't believe in them."

Nobody believes in abortion. Nobody believes that women should sometimes be made to have abortions. But we also don't believe that women should sometimes be made to have babies that they don't want and don't love.

All of us wish abortion didn't exist. It's not like people who are pro-choice think that all pregnant women should have abortions. We think that until there is better birth control and more teaching of sex education and relationship information, we have the right to offer the option of abortion to the pregnant woman.

Former U.S. surgeon general C. Everett Koop made a study and reported that abortion is a safe procedure, both emotionally and physically. He says he tried to find out where it's dangerous and damaging. He couldn't.

That's not to say there aren't some women who regret their decision. There are some women who become depressed and even need treatment. There are some women who become suicidal because of this and other factors. And there are complications that can occur.

Mixed Feelings

If you ask me, "Is an abortion totally safe?" I say, "This is like any other medical procedure. Things can go wrong. Perforation of the uterus, hemorrhage, all the complications associated with full-term pregnancy and labor occur here, too—only less frequently."

You have to decide for yourself, "How do I feel about having an abortion?" Most women have some mixed feelings. You wonder some about what that child would have been like had it gone to term. But most women do fine.

I also tell women of all ages, "Look, you can let somebody else make this decision. You can blame it on your mom. Blame it on your boyfriend. Blame it on us. But in the end, you're going to need to come to terms with it."

Some women cry, "I have no choice." Nobody can make you go into that room and have the abortion.

I say, "You always have a choice. You're in a bad situation and it looks like this is the way out for you. But you still have a choice. You can still walk out of here and stay pregnant. I will refer you to people who will help you do this."

We don't want to do abortions on women who are going to regret it.

Every Child Wanted

What advice do I have for teen males involved with a pregnancy? Let's say, she's just told you, "I think I'm pregnant."

What I've seen is that the couple does better if you—the guy—remain neutral. You hold back a little and give her some time. If you say, "I want you to have the abortion," she may feel you don't love her and won't love your child.

If you say, "I want you to have the baby," she may feel you want to trap her into being with you forever. What seems to work is if you say to her, "Okay, let's talk. Tell me how you feel about this pregnancy. What are you thinking? What do you feel would be the best decision for you?"

At a certain point—when she says, "What's the best decision for you?"—you should say how you feel and what you're willing to do to provide. You must be honest.

Planned Parenthood has a wonderful slogan: Every child wanted. That's our goal, too.

"The Best Solution Was Abortion."

Amy, 14 Years Old

I've had responsibility my whole life. My father's a farmer. He's an alcoholic, too. Starting when I was six, I had to take care of him. I basically lived in bars.

I remember fourth grade most of all. We would get up in the morning about seven o'clock. I'd go to school. When I got home, I'd go down and help Dad in the barn.

Then we'd go back up to the house, get changed, and we'd go out to a bar. We'd be there from—oh, geez, he got off work about six. We'd be in the bar from seven until three, four in the morning.

When the bar closes, I drag him out to the car. Get him in. Most of the time, I drive him home. He's too drunk even to see. I get him home by five in the morning and up by seven o'clock, two hours later.

It was that way every day. On weekends, forget it, 24 hours in the bar. It was amazing.

I had the responsibility of cleaning the house, cooking for my father and taking care of him. When he was sick, I stayed home and did his chores. I missed 53 days of school that year.

I met Mark when I was in eighth grade. He's older.

I liked being held, but I never really enjoyed the other

part. He said he'd pull out just before he came. That way I wouldn't get pregnant.

It didn't work.

I talked to my best girlfriend. I talked to the school nurse. She said in this state I didn't need a parent's permission to have an abortion. Why should I tell my dad? He barely knows I'm here. My mom left when I was little.

Screaming Voices

On Tuesday, my girlfriend and I cut school to go together for my abortion. I sat at a desk and heard them ask, "Is this your first abortion?" Then you have to fill out a questionnaire about your medical history, your periods and things like that. They go over it with you, to double-check everything.

Next they say, "Are you doing this of your own free will?" They make you write it on the bottom of that paper. You have to sign it, too.

When I was back in the waiting room, all of a sudden, you could hear these voices outside screaming, "Don't kill your baby! Come out with us. We'll take care of you. Those people only want your money. They don't care about you. They're trying to ruin your life!"

They were pounding on the door, shoving fliers under it.

Some of the girls started to cry. I got angry. I wanted a future! Were they going to help me take care of my father and a baby? I was brought up a fighter. I learned how to deal with problems. For me, the best solution was abortion.

The people at the clinic took us all into a room away from the noise. Nobody left. We all stayed to have the abortion.

No Sex, No Problem

I had this exam to see how far along I was—two months. You sit there until this guy takes blood from you. After all that, you put on a blue gown and these funny blue shoes. This lady takes your blood pressure. Then they send you to this other room where you watch TV until you're called.

They ask you how you want them to do it. You can be asleep or they can deaden you from the hips down. I wanted to be asleep. They stuck this needle in my wrist—the stuff that makes you go to sleep.

I was talking and they were talking. The next thing I knew, it was over. I was in the recovery room. They told me where I was.

You stay in the recovery room until you feel better. After about 10 minutes, they let you get up and walk around a little. They give you this pad, a Kotex, to put on for the bleeding. They had juice, graham crackers, and Tylenol for the pain. But I didn't take it.

They remind you, you shouldn't do a lot of exercising for two weeks, including no sex. I told them, "No problem."

PUBLIC STILL BACKS ABORTION, BUT WANTS LIM-ITS, POLL SAYS

Carey Goldberg with Janet Elder, *The New York Times*, 1/16/98

THE AMERICAN PUBLIC largely supports legalized abortion but says it should be harder to get and less readily chosen. In 1989, 48 percent thought an interrupted education was enough to justify a teenager's abortion; that dropped to 42 percent this year. Support remained overwhelming, however, for women who sought abortions because they had been raped, their health was endangered, or there was a strong chance of a defect in the baby.

People appeared receptive to the idea of a drug-induced abortion, now possible in the first seven weeks of pregnancy using a combination of drugs called RU-486, as an alternative to surgical abortion.

Kate Sullivan, Midwife
Boston, Massachusetts

Once you're aware you're pregnant, on an emotional level you start getting ready. You begin remarkable adjustments in yourself and in your ideas of what your life is going to be like. And then—if you're similar to one out of four or five females—you miscarry.

When you lose a pregnancy, if you feel you have family members or friends you want to tell this information, they often react by saying inappropriate things. "Oh, that's good," you hear. "You'll have a healthy baby some other time."

Because it's not unusual to be upset and grieve this loss, instead of that attitude, you hope for support and concern. If nothing else, you need to pay attention to your sadness. Try to let people know the truth of how you feel and be with those who will be nice to you. You are in a different stage of life than before you miscarried. Be tender and gentle with yourself.

Dividing and Multiplying

Most miscarriages happen in the first 12 weeks of pregnancy. What's amazing, though, is that no one really understands why they occur at all. Probably something goes wrong in basic cell division, the dividing and multiplying that takes place in the very early pregnancy once the egg and sperm join together.

Another common reason might be hormonal. At that moment you don't have enough female chemicals in your system to support the developing egg or placenta.

Sometimes you miscarry without knowing it, before you even realize you're pregnant. There's just heavy bleeding and the passage of something that might look like a tiny bit of tissue. But other times, it's both emotionally and physically painful. You have a lot of abdominal cramping.

Still other times, off and on you have spotting, but without cramping. Then later during a medical exam you discover you had a pregnancy that didn't progress in a healthy, viable way. In medical terms it's called a blighted ovum. When the pregnancy has stopped growing, but hasn't been passed from your body, it's called a missed abortion.

In some miscarriages, you continue to have cramping and bleeding. Your cervix opens up and parts, but not all of the tissue passes. In that case you need to have the medical procedure D&C, dilation and curettage.

Defective

After a miscarriage, many of you feel you're somehow "defective." Right away you try to become pregnant again, as if to make sure you're okay. Here are the facts.

One miscarriage does not increase your chance for

having another. After two in a row, you might have some medical situation to investigate—and definitely after three.

Some teenagers want a pregnancy to go away. Friends tell you about "things" that will work to help you miscarry. Don't follow their advice. You can make yourself really sick trying to force your body to miscarry.

"Without My Say-so, She Made an Appointment."

Written by
Tiana Baker, 17 Years Old
Argo Community High School, Summit, Illinois

Having an abortion wasn't by choice. I had to. The baby's father was thousands of miles away. I was emotionally depressed. I spent nights crying in my room, wondering why hadn't he called? Why could I never get in touch with him?

Come to find out he was in jail and didn't even know I was pregnant. After that, everything changed. I didn't eat. I slept all day. I barely wanted to go to school. I didn't want to talk to anybody.

Three months went by before I told my parents. Me and my father were kinda out of touch with each other. He didn't spend much time with me—still he took it the hardest. I watched him cry. It took days before he started making jokes, like calling me Big Momma.

Meanwhile, my mother was doing all she could to get me an abortion. Without my say-so, she made the appointment. The week I was scheduled, first I had to have an ultrasound. I don't think you should have to do that. It hurt to sit there and see a baby, yours, silent, floating in your stomach. And you're about to kill it.

I cried and cried. I am against abortion. I feared that it might be difficult to get pregnant later on. Plus it was mine and my parents had no interest in my feelings. For the first time in my life, I hated my mother.

Then the night before the abortion, she broke down crying and told me some things: "I was being foolish, Tiana," she said. "I'm sorry. I just didn't want you to mess up your life. After seeing the ultrasound, I know it's your child and your decision."

I chose the abortion.

My grandma came along to make sure I was going to be all right. I thought to myself, "I ain't gonna get bothered by it." But what a lie! To any teenage girl thinking about an abortion, weigh all the pros and cons—with the partner. Without him you won't get nowhere in decision making.

Pain and Irritation

During spring break the baby's father will see me for the first time since all this. He hates me, he says, because of the choice I made. "You should have gotten in touch," he says. What an asshole, right? I had been waiting and calling and calling and waiting, and he says that I'm the one.

Looking back, this is my best advice: Think first before you act. And you're better off having safe sex or no sex at all. The emotional pain and irritation you go through ain't worth it. To this day I regret the abortion.

Eunice Au, Editor of Newsletter "The Cross and the Rose"
Pregnancy Center, New Jersey

I'm against abortion.

I work as a volunteer at a pregnancy center. We're listed under "Clinics" in the yellow pages of the telephone directory. Girls call up and want to know information about abortions. They ask how much an abortion costs. Do we perform them?

We say, "We don't perform abortions here in the office."

You see, our goal is to persuade you not to have an abortion. If you knew ahead of time that was our goal, you might not come in. Across the country, there are places like this one with the same purpose and methods.

Once you're here, we give you a pregnancy test, show you videos about the issue, and find out why you want an abortion. Often we hear, "My parents will freak." Or, "It will screw up my life." Or, "I don't have the money." For most girls, though, the reason is that having a baby is inconvenient.

You want to deny you're pregnant. We say, "Imagine you wanted to be pregnant. You are happily married and have lots of money. You'd go, 'Yippee, I have a baby growing inside me.' It's just that today the circumstances are different. You can't, though, deny a baby is there."

If you have any religious background, we remind you that God says it's wrong to murder. Abortion is murdering a baby. You also face medical and psychological risks.

We know mostly you're scared. This is an upheaval to your life. We don't promise you any quick fixes. It's a lie if we say it's easy. But we can help you during and after the pregnancy through referrals to such places as prenatal clinics, drug programs and adoption agencies.

"I Had to Get a Judge to Say 'Okay' to My Abortion."

Heather, 20 Years Old

At the age of 14, I got sick with bronchitis. My mom took me to the doctor. He said, "We'll go have an X ray."

In the examining room there was one of those posters that read: "If you might be pregnant, let us know." All of a sudden, I remembered, "I haven't had my period!" To be honest, I hadn't even thought about pregnancy until I saw that sign.

You hear about it happening, but the girls who get pregnant are the ones always in trouble. I wasn't doing drugs. I wasn't out drinking. So why would I worry about getting pregnant? That's how I thought.

Of course, I was having sex without using birth control.

"I might be pregnant," I said to the doctor. "Can I have a pregnancy test without letting my mom know?"

My mom talked about sex, but when she did, she said it was wrong. I was too young.

But for me, boys and having crushes were in the picture by second grade. By eighth grade I started going with Tim. He was a year older. I liked that he was mature and had a good head on him. He was open and honest. He was always with me. This was big-time stuff, and his mother hated me.

I can still see it to this day. As I walked out of the doctor's office, he flashed a piece of paper. On it was the word "positive." I was pregnant. I got in the car and cried.

Madly in Love

First of all, I told Tim. We were both scared to death. We didn't know what to do. I wanted to close my eyes, go to sleep, and when I woke up, this would not be happening.

Then, like anybody else, I kind of fantasized about it. "This is wonderful. A baby!" I didn't, though, go off into that world of "Oh, Tim and I will get married. We'll have this baby." Sure I was madly in love with him and he was my first love. Still, I was 14 years old.

I worried to myself, "Be serious. There's no way I can support a baby. Mom would have to do it."

Then there was adoption. I felt I wasn't the right type

of person. If I did that, I'd still wonder today, "What is that baby doing? Are they loving parents?"

I talked to my girlfriends. One said she'd be there for me whatever I did. Another one thought babies are neat. She didn't believe in abortion, she told me.

To me, abortion was just a word. I didn't know anything. Tim and I agreed it was time to tell my mother. The problem was I didn't know how. We've always been close, but she had high expectations for me.

I hated school, but to her, education is everything. She doesn't have a college degree. So even though she always had a job, like executive secretary or office manager, it was a struggle raising me and my sister.

See, she and my dad divorced when I was five. He was an alcoholic and that broke them up. I don't remember much of him around the house. After he left, I only saw him a couple times a year. He was almost a stranger.

Anyway, I called my mom at work, so I wouldn't have to look at her face. "I have something to tell you," I said over the phone.

My mom didn't say things to make me feel worse than I already did. "What do you want to do, Heather?" she asked.

"I think I want to have an abortion," I said.

She called the Medical Women's Clinic to find out what I needed to do. When she hung up the phone, she couldn't believe it. In our state, before I could get an abortion, I had to tell both my biological parents or go to court to get a judge to say it was okay.

My mom was mad. She was the only supporting parent. She had total custody of me and my sister. She could sign for anything—except this.

I said, "I'm not going to tell Dad."

My mom and I agreed; I'd go to court. But that freaked me out. It was too personal a thing to tell some judge, a complete stranger.

I thought only bad people went to court. You know, like in the movies. And I really didn't have any idea about the court process. "I can't understand why we have to go to court," I told my mom. What could she do? It was the law.

Bucket in the Car

The clinic schedules both the appointment for court and the abortion on the same day. At that time, I'm sick. If there is cigarette smoke, I run to the bathroom. That morning we get up at this early hour and I'm sick, as usual. Tim, my mom and I drive to the clinic with a bucket in the car.

Once there, the three of us watch a video about what will happen that day. Then they do another pregnancy test and feel my stomach to tell how far along I am.

I talk to a counselor, too. We're alone. She asks me what concerns I might have. I want to know exactly what happens. Can I be put to sleep? Do they charge extra for that? Can I have somebody hold my hand? And then I ask about the pain.

"It's different for everybody," she says. "For some, it hurts a lot. For others, it's like very strong menstrual cramps."

She wants to know how I made my decision. Am I feeling good about it? Is anybody forcing me into this? If I want to back out, she says, this is my chance.

I feel comfortable with my decision. We talk about my future plans, including birth control. It's a neat session. Finally we talk about what will happen in court. By now it's 10 in the morning. I'm starving. You can't eat after midnight. With morning sickness, if you eat dry toast, the nausea goes away. I couldn't even eat that.

And I'm so scared.

We go to court, the three of us. We sit out in a big hallway, a bunch of us, other girls from clinics. Anybody can walk by and know why we're there: to see a judge for permission for an abortion.

Our privacy has been stripped away. It's awful.

First they call you in to talk to a court-appointed attorney. She asks all these personal questions. Why do I want to have an abortion? What is my family situation? Why don't I want to tell my father? Why won't I consider adoption?

It makes me feel worse, because I'm required to tell this person, another stranger.

Next I go wait in the courtroom. You get called in one by one to the judge's chambers. My mom goes in with me. And you know what? All he says is, "Hi. Why do you want an abortion?"

"I don't feel I'm ready to have a child. I want to go on to school."

"Fine," he says, scribble, scribble, and I'm out of there.

Severe Cramps

In the afternoon, I have the abortion. The waiting room is full. Some are having abortions. Some are supportive friends and relatives.

When I get called in, there's a lady who goes in with me. She says, "Will you please strip from the waist down and we'll begin." She's there for comfort and to talk to me. For about 30 seconds, my mind starts racing. I think, "What am I doing here? This isn't real."

The lady asks me questions about school and at the same time explains to me exactly what they're doing. She says, like, "They put the speculum in. And now they're going to give your cervix a shot. You're going to feel a little pinch." And that's just what happened. "Now they're going to put this in and turn on a machine. You're going to feel severe cramps." I have cramps, but they aren't bad.

Then they stop and scrape the insides of my uterus to make sure they got it all. They do this one more time and it's done. It's probably a total of five minutes. After that, I go sit in the waiting room, have toast and juice, and a half hour later—home.

I'm older now and looking back at that whole experience. Tim and I kept seeing each other for the next year or so. Then we grew apart. As far as the abortion, I have absolutely no regrets. Sometimes I think, wow, I would have a five-year-old! There's no way I could have done it.

What I think was awful, though, was the court experience. In a state where 50 percent of the minors are growing up in single-parent families, they say we need to tell both our parents. It's not fair.

INDUCED ABORTION

Facts in Brief, The Alan Guttmacher Institute, 1/97

EIGHTY-FOUR percent of all U.S. counties lack an abortion provider and 52 percent of abortion facilities provide services only through the 12th week of pregnancy.

Twenty-six states currently enforce parental consent or notification laws for minors seeking an abortion: Alabama, Arkansas, Delaware, Georgia, Iowa, Indiana, Kansas, Kentucky, Louisiana, Maine, Maryland, Michigan, Minnesota, Mississippi, Missouri, North Carolina, North Dakota, Nebraska, Ohio, Pennsylvania, Rhode Island, South Carolina, Utah, West Virginia, Wisconsin and Wyoming. Sixty-one percent of minors undergo the procedure with at least one parent's knowledge.

The U.S. Congress has barred the use of federal Medicaid funds to pay for abortions, except when the woman's life would be endangered by a full-term pregnancy or in case of rape or incest. Eighteen states pay for all or some abortions for poor women: Arkansas, California, Connecticut, Hawaii, Idaho, Illinois, Maine, Maryland, Minnesota, Montana, North Carolina, New Jersey, New Mexico, New York, Oregon, Vermont, Washington and West Virginia.

PART IV

KIDS TALKING ABOUT ADOPTiON, GUiLT, CHANGED MiNDS AND THE FUTURE

Judy Greene, Director, Birth Parent Services
Spence-Chapin
New York City, New York

There are two kinds of adoption: private and agency. With a private adoption, you go through an attorney. With an agency adoption, you go through a private agency—such as ours, Spence-Chapin, or a public one, such as a government agency, a county department of social services.

To find adoption agencies, look in the yellow pages of the telephone directory under "Adoption" or "Social Services." School counselors, women's health clinics and teen parenting networks can help you, too.

Those of us at adoption agencies are not here to talk you into or out of anything. What we try to do is prepare you for the choices you need to make.

Most often you hope you're not pregnant. That means a lot of our clients don't come to us until the sixth, seventh or eighth month of pregnancy. You wait beyond the time you can have an abortion. Then you're faced with raising the baby yourself or
placing the baby for adoption. And you're not sure how you feel about it. Some say you see adoption as selfish, irresponsible and abandoning the baby.

If you feel that way, I ask, "What does a good parent do?"

Usually I hear, "A good parent takes care of the baby. You make sure it gets fed, clothed, and loved—and that it's taught the things it needs to know."

I say to you, "Isn't that what you're doing? A good parent provides for a child. You're providing a loving, adoptive family." You should not feel guilty if you don't feel ready to be a parent. It's okay to want to do the things that teenagers do.

Bad Feelings

The sooner you contact an adoption agency, the more we can help you. For example, we talk about decision making. We answer your questions.

One question we hear a lot is: Do my parents have to know about the pregnancy and adoption? We strongly suggest you involve your parents, especially if you live at home.

Most teenagers think, "My parents will kick me out of the house." Rarely does that happen. Sure, there's some anger and shock. But we hear from most girls that the parents are supportive.

However, some of you grow up with abusive parents. There's nothing in the law that says they have to know. In fact, this is one of the few situations where you, a minor, can sign a contract—the paper giving up the child. Legally, the child is yours.

Another question we hear is: Does *he* have to know? Many times it was not a serious relationship. Or it's over, and now you've found out you're pregnant. No matter who did the breaking up, you've got bad feelings.

We help you separate out those feelings and think about how this child is going to feel growing up when it says, "What did my daddy look like? What ethnic background am I? Can I inherit any medical condition from him?" For the baby's future, we need to get information about both parents.

Let's say the birth father doesn't want to get involved at all. We say to you, the birth mother, "Could you take this medical form, leave off the name and have him or his family fill it out?" In many states, though, you have to name him. In turn, birth fathers are increasingly getting more rights.

When you fill out the form, you should be open and up-front. If you're crack-addicted, let us know. If you have childhood diabetes in your family, let us know. If this baby is the result of incest, let us know. We may have to say to you, we don't have any families that can accept the baby at this moment. But we'll work with you to find an organization or a family that will take this child.

If you come to us, we ask you what you want in an adoptive family. Maybe you say, "I want them to be Catholic. I want them to be college graduates, artistic, athletic and have a dog."

We then give you information about several families that meet your criteria. The material often includes how the couple met and why they were attracted. It gives a physical description, education and jobs. In some cases, you might want to meet the potential adoptive parents. These meetings don't always go the way you expect, but they're all wonderful.

Some agencies and private lawyers feel that teenage birth mothers aren't mature enough to make the decision on which family is right for their baby. They don't want you to meet. Ask the agency or lawyer you're thinking of going through, "What's your policy on this?"

Today, more and more birth mothers and adoptive parents know one anothers' names and addresses. After the baby is born, some even keep meeting maybe once a week to once a year.

Changed Minds

Pregnancy often makes you feel fat, angry, frustrated and sad. Why me, you wonder?

One day, though, a baby is born. You're dealing with your flesh and blood. It's a different set of feelings. This is a crucial time for the birth mother.

In most private adoptions, through an attorney, the birth mother signs the papers in the hospital. The baby is discharged and goes immediately to the adoptive family.

With Spence-Chapin and many other agency adoptions, we give the birth mother a few days or even a few months where the baby is put in temporary child care.

You've just gone through childbirth. It can be difficult under the best circumstances. You're under medication. You have incredible highs and lows. This is not always the right time to make such a serious choice. You need to distance yourself to make sure this is what you want.

The decision to place a child in adoption—or raise a child by yourself—is one you have to live with for the rest of your life. We want you to feel good about it.

At this point, the vast majority of birth mothers change their minds. They keep the baby.

For those who do turn to adoption, state laws vary about the formal procedure for signing what's called surrender papers. What you should know, though, is that once you sign the papers, there is no easy way to get the child back if you change your mind.

It's painful and expensive for everyone. It would be much better if you take extra weeks to make sure your decision is solid.

I think some people feel, "Oh, I'll never get over this." The truth is, while you don't forget, you learn to live with it. And with an agency's help, you learn to live with it in a much better way.

"It Was Too Late for an Abortion."

Emily, 16 Years Old

David's the first person I ever slept with. He's different than most guys. He isn't self-centered, always talking about himself. He isn't macho. He's just nice.

For months, I told myself a million reasons why there was no way I could be pregnant, especially since David used a condom. Finally, I knew I had to move on it. At the time, I was not going to tell my parents. I was set on getting an abortion.

I cut school and went to a women's health clinic. I'd never been to a gynecologist before. Once inside, I was shuffled around to different people. First, one lady filled out an application, another did a blood and urine test, another did the examination and another talked to me.

The doctor said, "You're 21 weeks pregnant. How could you let this go so late?! We can't legally do this."

I was hysterical. In my mind, I wanted it to be over. I didn't want anybody to know. I had tried to make decisions by myself with David.

A counselor said, "If you still want to get it done, you could go to New York State. It's legal there up to 24 weeks." The more she told me, the more freaked I got: Be prepared for demonstrators outside. What it is, more or less, is they give you a saline solution that forces you to miscarry.

I'd been a wreck about getting an abortion, borrowing the money from David's best friend, and now I was, like, forget it.

I told my parents. David told his. All of them were upset, but they were more worried about him and me. How could we go through all those months hurting ourselves without telling them?

A Future

My dad came into my room and said, "We're going to figure everything out."

"I'm so sorry," I told him. "I never wanted to disappoint anyone."

David was scared to death my parents would hate him. But they knew and loved him. They never gave either of us ultimatums. Finally, me, my mother, my father, and David sat down and talked about options.

"If you decide to keep the baby," my mom said, "you could still go to school. You could still go to college. We'll help you as much as we can with watching her. We'll support you financially as much as possible."

"Keeping it is not an option," I said. One or two friends had done that. It was not the way I wanted my life or a baby's life to be. It was unfair. Then I felt selfish: All I could think about was myself.

Still, I wanted a future. The baby would be more like my sister than my child. My parents would wind up raising her. Everyone's life at home, my sister and brother's, would be affected, too.

My mom said her doctor, a GYN, got hundreds of letters from couples asking if he knew of women who are pregnant and don't want to keep it. Finding a home for my baby—a white baby—would be no problem, he told her.

I felt the baby move.

The doctor wrote a letter to school, saying I needed home tutoring. I was "fatigued." I didn't want to have to deal with telling my friends. I just couldn't.

My mom went to see the lawyer the doctor suggested. How does adoption work? she wanted to know. What were my rights?

A Meeting

In the beginning, I didn't want to meet Wendy and Harlow, the couple the doctor and lawyer said wanted to adopt the baby. David did. He wanted to know what kind of people they were.

Then I changed my mind. The word came back—they didn't want to see us. I got annoyed. I said, "I don't mean to sound like a bitch, but I'm giving them something they can never have. I don't think I'm asking that much." They set up a meeting.

It was awkward at first. Nobody knew what to say. I told them, "Please, don't feel like you're being interrogated. You're the people we've decided on. We just want to know what you're like."

After talking a while, you could tell they really liked as well as loved each other. They liked doing stuff together. And then they asked things about David and me.

They said they'd tell the child about meeting us.

You know, David was wonderful during this whole thing. Everyone was so worried about me that none of our parents saw how much he was going through. He was always calming me down. And he was scared that,

God forbid, something might happen to me. I tried to let him know how much I appreciated all his support.

The doctor said, "Whenever your contractions are five minutes apart for an hour or your water breaks, go to the hospital."

The Twinges

I was in bed, staring at the ceiling, when the twinges started. I woke up my mom and said, "We should go!"

"Relax," she told me.

I called David and told his mom I was ready. My dad walked the dog. I started throwing up. My mom said, "Don't worry. There's no more pain than bad cramps."

That's not true! I was in agony.

After the birth of a baby girl, I felt lousy. I'd had an episiotomy. I had stitches and stuff. I was exhausted.

The nurses on the floor knew about the adoption. They put me in a room at the end of the wing by myself. That way, I didn't have to deal with other women and their new babies.

The lawyer wanted me to sign some papers. He'd take the baby to the couple. I was nervous. I went down to the nursery with David to see her.

Later, when I asked, a nurse brought the baby to my room. I looked at her. I played with her. I didn't hold her. I thought that was best. I didn't want to get attached to her.

I started to get depressed. I could hear women with their babies, giggling and cooing. I remember crying, saying to David, "I don't know what I want to do."

"You need time to decide, Emily."

They all knew I was getting depressed. It was agreed the baby would be put in boarding care for a month while I thought about my decision.

My mom said, "You may not want to keep her as far

as how you'd have to adjust your life. But, if you're going to hurt every day because you miss her so much...."

The whole time I was pregnant, I was convinced it was a boy. Having a girl made the decision harder for me. What if I never had another girl? What if I couldn't have any more children?

Meanwhile, the lawyer kept reminding me these people were both making over $100,000 a year. They could financially care for her better than I could.

It wasn't as if she'd starve if I raised her. I was envious of them for being able to have her. I wished I could have been married. I wished it was later in my life when I could have kept her. In the end, I felt I had no choice but to give her up. In my heart, as much as I was sad, I knew it was for the best.

A month after I gave birth, I went in front of a judge to sign the surrender papers. She asked me if I understood everything. At that point, I was giving up my legal rights to the baby, but I did have 30 days to appeal it.

For the first 30 days when my baby was in boarding care, I could have changed my mind and taken her just like that. The judge said, "After you sign these papers, if, for some reason you change your mind, you will have to appeal it and go to court. The court will then decide who gets the baby."

She said again, if I signed this, that has to be final. I wasn't thinking, "Ohmigosh, I'm signing her away." I just did it. I was anxious for us both to get on with our lives.

I Cried

It's been six months now. In daily life, David and I go to school, go to work, things like that. When I'm upset about other things, I start to think about the baby.

Yesterday I was watching a TV show where a woman

just found out she was pregnant. I cried. I cried for me and the baby who will never know me. Will she hate me?

Today, Eight Years Later

Eight years have passed since Emily and I talked. These are her feelings today:

I'm 25. I graduated from college. David and I are still friends, but I'm engaged to someone else. My fiancé knows what happened. He's supportive, even though I don't think you understand unless you went through it.

For the first year, the whole thing was on my mind every day. I was nervous about having sex. I couldn't separate it from the fact I might become pregnant again. Basically David and I had a platonic relationship.

I didn't regret my decision, but I felt guilty and selfish. While the baby's welfare was a big concern, mine was more important. And I had made it this horrible secret.
I began to realize it wasn't fair to the baby I gave birth to. I had her and she was part of my life. It wasn't something I should be ashamed of. I started to tell my best girlfriends.

Finally I went to a therapist. She said I shouldn't wallow in what happened, worrying is she sick? Did she die? What if I'd done this or that? I put up a stop sign against all the "what-ifs."

She had me go to the mall to look at 16-year-old girls. "See how they act," she said. "You think of yourself as more mature, as if you were an adult back then. You're so hard on yourself for a decision you made as best you could."

I try to be objective. I hope to hear from her someday, but if she doesn't feel compelled to find me, I'll assume she's settled and happy.

"You Can't Just Live on Love."

Dawn Lee,
16 Years Old

AT THIRTEEN I MOVED IN WITH MY DAD AND STEPMOM. BUT THE STREETS WERE BETTER THAN WHAT WAS GOING ON IN THAT HOUSE. I RAN AWAY.

IN SCHOOL I'M DUMB AS A BRICK. STREETWISE I'M A WINNER.

DAWN, CHECK IT OUT— WE GOT SOME GOOD STUFF.

WHEN I FOUND OUT I WAS PREGNANT, IT WAS TORTURE. I WAS SLEEPING WITH SO MANY DIFFERENT GUYS— AND WITHOUT PROTECTION. I CALLED MY REAL MOM, EVEN THOUGH WE'D HAD PROBLEMS.

HI MOM. I'M SAFE, BUT I'VE GOT A PROBLEM.

WHAT IF I HAVE AIDS AND GIVE IT TO MY BABY?!

STILL IT WASN'T LIKE I HAD LOTS OF CHOICES WHERE TO GO. I ENDED UP BACK LIVING WITH HER.

STAY IN YOUR ROOM! I DON'T WANT MY FRIENDS TO SEE YOU!

MOM WAS ASHAMED OF ME ONE MINUTE... ...AND THE NEXT MINUTE...

AWWW! I CAN FEEL IT KICK!

THEN OUT OF THE BLUE SHE TOLD ME SHE PICKED OUT A SUITABLE COUPLE, RON AND KELLY, FOR ADOPTION.

MY MOM SET THIS UP. BUT I CAN'T DO IT.

GET IN THE CAR! *©$£!!

My MOM SAID WE COULDN'T STAY WITH HER, SO THE TWO OF US MOVED IN WITH MY DAD AND STEPMOM.

THE DAY SHE TOOK HER· FIRST STEP, I FOUND OUT I WAS PREGNANT AGAIN. WHEN I TOLD THE GUY I WAS SEEING THEN, HE BLEW UP.

WHAT I DID WAS THE MOST UNSELFISH THING I COULD THINK OF. I LET THAT SAME COUPLE, RON AND KELLY, ADOPT MY **NEW BABY.**

I CAN'T TAKE CARE OF YOU RIGHT.

FOR THE LAST TWO MONTHS OF MY PREGNANCY DAUN LEA AND I LIVED WITH THEM.

WHEN HE WAS BORN, I WOULDN'T EVEN HOLD HIM.

SINCE I CAN'T BE HIS MOM, I'LL GIVE HIM SOMETHING HE CAN'T THROW AWAY— HIS NAME... TRAVIS MICHAEL, AFTER HIS DAD.

SOB

YOU CAN VISIT, AND BE HIS "AUNTIE DAWN"!

I FEEL SO BAD, CHOOSING ONE CHILD AND LETTING THE OTHER GO.

81

YOU CAN'T JUST LIVE ON LOVE, I TOLD MYSELF. THAT COUPLE GIVES HIM WHAT I CAN'T: A SAFE, HAPPY ENVIRONMENT, AND MY DAUGHTER? I ONLY MAKE $300 A WEEK. MY DAD AND STEPMOM ARE RAISING HER.

I'VE RUN AWAY AGAIN. I'M TRYING TO GET MY LIFE TOGETHER, I GOT A PLACE OF MY OWN, A NEW WARDROBE, AND I WANT TO PUBLISH MY POEMS.

NOT A DAY GOES BY WHEN I DON'T THINK OF THEM.

WHAT DOESN'T KILL YOU MAKES YOU STRONGER.

IDA MARX BLUE SPRUCE

Beth, Adoptive Mother,
Private Independent Adoption

Four years ago, my husband and I adopted a baby. We named him Lucas. Now we're trying to adopt another child.

Like most adoptive parents, first we went through such a nightmare trying to have a baby. I had miscarriages, ectopic pregnancies and years of tests. Not being able to make a baby is heartbreaking.

Finally, we decided to try to adopt. Instead of going through an agency where you wait and wait for them to call you, we went to an attorney who specializes in independent adoptions. He told us what to do.

Financially Secure Couple

We take out personal ads in newspapers. They say: "Happily married, financially secure couple looking to adopt a newborn. Please call the following number. Let us help you."

We have a phone number just for those calls. When that phone rings, we're scared. We want this baby more than anything in the world. And we don't know who's calling. Are you for real?

You should understand something important. This method of adoption has become well known. A lot of not-very-together people make a lot of phony calls. These kinds of calls are cruel.

Because of them, sometimes the person who calls—maybe someone like you—is questioned a little too closely. Just remember, we only want to know the truth. It's so important that you're honest.

In this first phone call, we ask for a few details. What happened? Why are you giving up the baby? How's your health? Have you been to the doctor? Are you sure you want to do this? Describe yourself. Describe the birth father, if you can. Not all birth mothers are sure who the father is. That's okay, too.

I know you're probably nervous answering these questions. You think, "These successful adults are going to be sitting in judgment of me. And here I am pregnant!"

Neither of us on this end of the phone thinks you're stupid or horrible. We've all had a sex life. Maybe we didn't get pregnant by accident, but the reason might have been that we couldn't get pregnant at all.

Usually we hear from someone who's about four or five months pregnant. And yes, you're going through a rough time. Frankly, though, I respect you for trying to make the best decision for the future of the child. You're responsible and caring.

Callers ask me questions, too. I hear, "Will you tell the child that he's adopted?"

"Of course," I answer. Lucas is four and we have begun talking to him about it. We describe it to him in the most loving way. We say he didn't grow in my belly. He grew in someone else's. She loved him and couldn't take care of him.

As he gets older, we'll give him more details.

Some callers worry that we'll tell the baby that you didn't care. Or that you were a bad person. No adoptive parent would ever do that. It's not good for the child.

One young woman asks a special question. She wants to see if I'm capable of loving a baby I didn't make. She says, "Describe how you felt when they put your son in your arms."

"It was the most extraordinarily happy moment in my life," I answer.

Get Grilled

After this first conversation, we give you our attorney's number to call. That's where you should expect to really get grilled. The attorney asks about everything from your nationality to any drug use during pregnancy.

There's a long list of medical problems he checks off, including anything else we should know about your own family and the birth father's family. Does the birth father know about this, and if so, how does he feel? Would he be willing to sign the appropriate forms?

Unless you're in the same city, this interview usually is not done in person. At some point, though, our attorney sends you to another attorney in your hometown to make sure everything is in order.

And certainly, before any money is given to you to help out, say, with medical expenses, basic living costs and so on, you have to go to a doctor. You do this to confirm the pregnancy. You see, some people call and pretend they're pregnant just to get money.

You can call adoptive parents and talk to them and not be sure about adoption. You can talk to an attorney and not be sure. But once you commit to adoption, once you're heading down that road, you're involving other people. You have to come to terms with what you're doing.

In our own way, with our financial and emotional commitment, we're pregnant with you. We're expecting this baby, too. Last time we bought stuff for a nursery and kept it in my friend's garage. Up until we actually had the baby in our arms, we were terrified it was not going to happen, that the woman would change her mind.

This time, the young woman is due in six weeks. And between you and me, I don't know if she's going to give us the baby. While we're very sympathetic to her indecision and fears, we're terrified again. We feel vulnerable.

I start feeling depressed over not having been able to do this magical thing—have a child—myself. I pull myself up short with the following thought:

If God on high came down and said, "It was a big mistake. You can make your own children. In fact, you can make three of them. The only thing is, you have to give up Lucas. He can't be in your life." I absolutely wouldn't do it.

There is nothing in the world, no promise of any kind that would make me want to give up this son. There's no difference between the way I love Lucas and the way birth parents love a child.

Today, Eight Years Later

Here is an update from Beth:
We did get ripped off by that woman. It was horrible. She lied about the pregnancy, about the father, about so many things.

But then we tried again and found a lovely couple who didn't feel they could give a baby what they wanted to. Now we have two handsome, intelligent cheerful sons. They're what kids should be. Lucas, the 12-year-old, can be obnoxious, and the seven-year-old, Joshua, can be demanding. They are both great and very much loved.

Last year Lucas asked to see a picture of his birth mother. He asked why she did this, and I told him the truth: "It's a tremendous job. She couldn't do it. You are more important than a romantic idea of keeping a baby."

In no way does he resent what she did. He sees how much kids cost, the work I do and the things involved. He appreciates that she wanted to give him a life. Also, we live in a community with other adopted kids. He doesn't feel out of place.

Joshua to date is unconcerned. But I'm always ready to answer his questions.

PART V

KIDS

TALKING ABOUT

FOSTER CARE,
A STEPDAD,
DRUGS AND JAiL

"My Stepdad Got Me Pregnant."

Stephanie, 16 Years Old

When I was a kid, I lived with my mother, my stepdad, my stepbrother and my half sister. By the time I was 11, my stepfather was coming into my bedroom and raping me. If I told anyone, he said he'd do the same thing to my little sister.

Two years later, I got pregnant. He was the father.

To deal with it, I pretended it wasn't true. By the time I was six or seven months pregnant, kids at school would say, "Stephanie, are you pregnant?"

"What?" I'd say. "Are you crazy? I've just gained weight." Finally my mother said, "Go have yourself tested." I did, and I was pregnant.

What I didn't know was someone had made an anonymous call to social services about the stuff going on at home. They sent a social worker to school to talk to me. I didn't want to tell anybody. I didn't want to uproot the whole family.

Someone from social services went to my house too. They arrested my stepdad that very day.

Liar!

I leave school, take the bus home, and walk into this. My half sister starts screaming at me, "I hate you." Andrew, my stepbrother, says, "Why did you say it was Dad?" This is his son. He can't believe it.

When my mom gets home from work, she starts screaming, too, "You're a liar! A liar!"

I feel terrible. I cry and cry.

A Slave

At school, everybody stared at me. I knew they were saying I was disgusting. I didn't care. My close friends accepted me. I just kept going to school until a week before the baby was due.

The doctor said my amniotic fluid was very low. The baby didn't want to come out. They wanted to induce labor—make it start. They would give me medication to bring on contractions.

At three in the afternoon, they took me off the medication. At four o'clock, my water broke. I said to my mother, "I feel like I have to go to the bathroom." I was in such pain.

Then, all of a sudden, there was the baby's head. They shoved me into the delivery room and the doctor came in at a dead run. Ten minutes later my baby was born. She had a full head of red hair, and I named her Rusty.

After I was home from the hospital for two weeks, my mom said, "I can't take this anymore. I want social services to put you in a foster home."

WHAT!?

It was like she kept me at home while I was pregnant. After Rusty was born, I could go on my own. A caseworker from social services said, "Stephanie, we have a nice home for you with a foster care family."

It was a young couple. They were only 22 and 23 themselves. They had three little kids. The state would pay them $300 a month each for Rusty and me, a total of $600.

That night, I packed my stuff by myself. Next I packed what little I had for Rusty. In the morning we left to move in with that couple.

Within weeks, they were using me like a slave. Wash dishes, cook, scrub the showers, wax the floor, clean the windows. On weekends, they had a bigger list of things to do. Everything had to be spotless.

Rusty would cry. I'd let her go. The husband would yell, "Pick her up." But I thought picking up a baby every time teaches a bad lesson. And I wanted to raise her the way I thought best.

Three months after I had Rusty, I went back to school. I was in bad shape, tired and feeling guilty. I thought I should stay home with her, but how could I do that and get an education? I wanted to excel!

I'd come home with schoolwork, then stay up half the night 'cause Rusty was colicky. By then she was crying all the time. "Pick her up," the husband would holler.

Only Probation

My caseworker stopped by to see how I was doing. She told me my stepfather had moved back in with my mom. Charges were brought against him, but he only got probation. "Don't worry," she said. "Things will be okay."

"What do I tell Rusty when she asks about her daddy?" I'd think to myself.

I was 13 when I got pregnant. I was 14 when I had Rusty. I was 15 now and I wanted to have my own home. To learn how, I took some classes in independent living skills.

"We'll find you a different foster family, instead," the caseworker said.

And they did. The problem was the husband had been in Vietnam. He had flashbacks. He'd cry out in pain, like someone was kicking him. His wife was religious. She wanted him to go to this place where they get the Lord back into you.

Meanwhile, I felt like I never slept. I was always doing for Rusty, going to school or studying. I never went out with friends. I had responsibility.

The only person I talked to during this whole time was Rusty, and with her I'd just sit there and cry. "I have to do well in school. It's our best hope for the future."

She listened to me. She cried with me. It was like she understood me. When I stopped crying, she stopped crying. When I brought home my report card and was on the honor roll, we smiled together.

My foster mother thought I needed to get out a little. "Why not find a part-time job?" she said. "Taco Bell needs help." I started working about five hours a night, four nights a week and weekends. At times I was working 30 to 35 hours a week. I loved it, but it was killing me.

Rusty went from day care to a nighttime baby-sitter.

My foster mother said, "She's a disaster. Every time you leave the house, she screams her bloody head off."

She was two by now. She wouldn't sleep at night. When I was home, she followed me around like a lost puppy. We were both irritable. My caseworker was bugging me about parenting classes. I was getting, like, I can't handle this anymore.

On my 16th birthday, I bought myself a car.

I came home from work and my foster mother told me she had to spank Rusty to get her to bed. I looked at her and saw bruises. Bruises! I was upset.

My caseworker and my foster mother said, "Stephanie, cut back on your work hours."

"Okay," I said, even though I needed money for Rusty's diapers and clothes, and now car payments. That worked for a week. I had to have my work. My work was my sanity. I was learning management, something good for my future.

I went to social services. "Look," I said, "I want to put Rusty in foster care by herself. I think it will be better for her. I'll catch my breath. I'll go live with my girlfriend and her mother."

No Nothing

It was a hot day. I dressed Rusty in a white jumper with a sailboat on it. I put her in the car and took her to another foster family. The new foster father came over to the car, opened the door and unhooked the car seat. He took her away. No hug. No kiss. No good-bye. No nothing.

Rusty, my little two-year-old, turned back and looked at me, like, "What's going on?" I drove to my girl-friend's looking through my tears, flooded in the face with reality.

Janie Gore Golan,
Director of Adoption Resource Consultants, Inc.
Plano, Texas

When I was 16, I did some research in a hospital emergency room. One day a doctor said, "I want you to see this baby."

"What's the matter with her?" I asked.

"The mother was on angel dust. Her baby was born without a brain. That's called anencephalic."

The next day the baby died.

That's when I began to learn the effects of drugs on a fetus and a child.

Today, when a pregnant teen tells us, "Oh, I only smoke a little marijuana," we ask if you know that smoking anything has an impact on the fetus. And if you're talking about heroin or crack, drinking four-packs of wine coolers or even using over-the-counter drugs like diet pills, you are a walking time bomb, and so is your baby.

Crack, FAS and Frustration

Every day something new develops in the fetus. Your baby's heart, lungs, liver, kidneys—all the vital organs, and its arms and legs—are formed during the first trimester, the first 12 weeks of pregnancy. Any type of drug, with the probable exception of those prescribed by a doctor, may affect that growth in a bad way.

Kids may be born with too small or too large a head, microcephalic or macrocephalic. They can be born with one eye higher than the other. They can be born without kidneys. They can develop cerebral palsy.

When you use crack or cocaine during a pregnancy, the child you give birth to at first may look healthy. Then a week later, he or she could have the shakes and be irritable. And by irritable, I mean screaming and unable to sleep.

Crack babies don't tolerate feedings well. They are extremely demanding. Often they're not able to respond or give love in return. Some medical professionals say, "It's poverty that causes these problems. Anyway babies born addicted to alcohol are more messed up physically and psychologically than those born addicted to crack."

Regardless, you can't forget that doing illegal drugs during a pregnancy is never going to help you or your child. Children whose mothers drink during the pregnancy can be born with what's called fetal alcohol syndrome, FAS. You look at a child with FAS—you see the eyes are very small. The child appears to be sullen. The children might also be mentally retarded.

With two to three drinks a day, a pregnant woman increases the chances of giving birth to a child with FAS by 11 percent. Four or more drinks, it's 19 percent. The more you drink, the greater the danger.

If you're using drugs or drinking, see a doctor. Level with him or her. That person may be able to get you the kind of help you need. However, many pregnant teens become frustrated by the lack of agencies willing to work with those doing drugs.

Your choices narrow. Drug-exposed children are exceedingly difficult to place in adoption. Your baby may be taken from you and end up rotting in foster care.

CLINTON TO APPROVE SWEEPING SHIFT IN ADOPTION/FOSTER CARE

Katherine Q. Seelye, *The New York Times*, 11/17/97

THE NEW LEGISLATION marks a fundamental shift in child-welfare philosophy, away from a presumption that everything should be done to reunite children with their birth parents, even if the parents have been abusive. The legislation would instead give more weight to the child's health and safety. The numbers of children in foster care climb every year and are now up 89 percent from 1982 levels.

"My Boyfriend Was Jailed for Child Abuse."

Judy, 17 Years Old

On New Year's Eve, I was with this guy, Eddie. I met him at the bowling alley the month before. He was visiting a friend in town. I thought he was nice. He laughed all the time.

I was curious about sex. It was one of those things. I just wanted to do it. An hour later, we went home.

When I missed a second period, I knew something was up. First, I thought, "This can't happen." Then I decided, if I'm pregnant, I'm pregnant. I can't give it back.

I told Eddie, and he said he'd buy me a pregnancy test. He never got around to it. Then I told my sister, and added, "You have a big mouth. I want to keep it secret from Mom for a while."

Later that day, me and my sister were in the bathroom trying to curl our hair. We got in a fight. She got so mad she went running to Mom saying, "Judy's pregnant."

Mom screamed upstairs, "You're what?!" Well, she just threw a hissy fit. "How'd this happen?" she wanted to know.

"How do you think?" I said.

I felt abortion was cruel. I was going to have this baby. Mom was kind to me once she got over the shock. She rented me a little apartment to live in.

Pretty soon, though, Eddie and I got in this big fight. He broke up with me. He just didn't bother to let me know.

See, there was this other girl, Donna. Her boyfriend kept beating on her. Eddie went to beat the beep out of him. After that, the two of them, Eddie and Donna, got together.

When I found out about all this, I told him, "I don't know what the hell you're doing. All I know is you were going with me. Now you're going out with someone else. No one does that to me."

Eddie said, "Well, if we're broke up, now I can go with Donna."

Left the State

I was five months pregnant. Morning sickness sucked. Once that was over, it was cool. When you're pregnant, people are nice to you. No one gets on your case.

I started dating again. And guys loved that I was pregnant. They wanted to see how it felt to go out with a pregnant girl!

Then I got a call from a social worker. Because I was on welfare, they wanted to know about the baby's father. They had to have it for paternity papers. The only thing I knew was his name. I told them the truth: "I heard he left the state."

By then, I had started dating Max. None of my friends liked him. He hadn't gone past 11th grade. I dropped out of school, too.

I wanted to spend time with my sister. Max wouldn't let me. But he was there for me. He showed up. He came to the hospital for the birth of Shannon.

For about a month, I stayed with Max at his home. It was his mother, me, him and the baby. Then we moved three different times. Mainly, we stayed with friends for a while.

Max had a job at a pizzeria. I made him help with the baby, too. He'd get up in the morning, give her a bath, feed and change her. That's when I'd get up.

He started complaining, "That's your job."

"I get up in the middle of the night. You try that once in a while," I told him.

One morning, all I know was Max was changing the baby like usual. He picked her up by the arm and went to stick his other hand underneath her butt. By the time he started to do that, the baby wiggled around and started screaming.

She kept screaming, really long. Shannon has a high-pitched scream. Usually, you pick her up, hold her and she stops crying. This time she didn't. And she wouldn't move her arm. I knew something was wrong.

The doctor took a look and said her arm was broke. Then out of nowhere, protective services got involved. They came to the hospital and asked, "What happened?" We told them the story.

I can't remember exactly what they said—something about neglect and abuse. "We've got to take your baby away, put her in a foster home," they said.

I started crying, "Give me my baby back." She was just three months old. I was being a good mother.

We went home. It was hard seeing the crib there and everything. I couldn't get to sleep that night. The doctor gave me "dry pills" to take so the milk in my boobs wouldn't hurt that much.

Mumbo-jumbo Talk

There was a hearing. I had to go in to the court and talk to a judge. He asked me a bunch of stuff, like, "Explain what happened." He said, "You're going to have to go to parenting class."

Then the judge said I had to see Shannon one hour twice a week and all this mumbo-jumbo talk that they do. Next Max had to go to court. It was scary.

Judges always put different words in there. You say it and they say it and it comes out different. The judge said, "How could you do that to a baby? You'll spend 30 days in jail—child abuse, second degree."

I've seen babies fall off changing tables all the time. They break a leg or something. I don't see protective services jumping on them. It's just like with certain people they do.

I think they came after me 'cause I'm a teenager. It isn't any of their business. I should be able to raise my kid the way I want. I hate it when people get involved in your problems when you don't want them to.

When Max was in jail, I wrote him a letter. I said it wasn't working out between us. He wrote me, saying, "Can we be friends?"

Now he's out and he won't even talk to me. He's got a loose screw somewhere. I wanted him to say, "I'm sorry for what happened to the baby."

Then I could say, "Yeah, right." But I didn't hear any apologies. Sometimes I think about what to tell Shannon about her dad. I'll say, "Yeah, you do have a dad. Somewhere around these United States. Someday you might see him. It just didn't work out between us."

To me, a guy's a guy. You've got to expect that from them. I won't throw my anger up to my kid.

But it's weird now. I live by myself in a downstairs apartment. I don't even have cable TV. I'm lonely. I go back to court September 19th. I should be able to get my baby back within that month. Shannon's a year old now.

I pick her up from the foster home. She's walking all over the place. I got a stroller so I can take her over to my friends to show her off.

I'd like to have a boyfriend. I like being with someone. It's fun—share the laughter, share the joy. What's
important, too, is I want to be a good parent. That's all
I've got to say.

PART VI

KIDS

TALKING ABOUT
PARENTiNG FOREVER,
A MAD GiRL AND
MAKiNG BABiES

"We'd Better Last Forever."

Susan, 16 Years Old

I don't like being alone. I've always had a boyfriend. But back when I was 14, before I met Peter, boyfriends sometimes meant trouble. We partied, did drugs, cut school. One month I was in class for only a day.

My parents always compared me to my "perfect" older brother. I didn't care. I wanted to do what I wanted to do.

Then Peter and I started to get serious. He picked me up every day. We walked each other to classes. We went to lunch together. After school we'd go to work and meet right after.

At night we either ate supper at my house or his. Then we'd go into his downstairs bedroom. We'd watch TV and whatever else. Every time we came upstairs, his mom and dad said, "You're going to have a problem that you're not going to be able to deal with."

Every time Peter said, "Don't worry."

We'd been going together for about eight months when I got pregnant. Since I couldn't get the nerve to tell my mother, Peter followed her into the kitchen and said, "Susan's seven weeks pregnant."

She shook her head and said, "Stupid kids. You should know better." She came into the living room where I was and said, "There's going to be no abortion."

"Fine. I want to have my own baby, anyway," I said. Then I started to cry. "I feel bad because I hurt you again."

"Don't feel bad for me," she said. "Feel bad for yourself."

Next we went over to Peter's. His dad was sleeping in front of the TV. His mom was sewing up a shirt. "I'm going to tell you something you're not going to like," Peter said.

She knew right away. She told me I had to stay in school. Then she gave us both a hug, cried a little and said I'd better go see the doctor.

The Worst Pain

I went to my doctor's office about once every month. Near the end, I went every other week. At first he gave me lots of pamphlets to read—like, if you're smoking, your baby is, too. What the risks are when somebody young gets pregnant: Sometimes you can't go full term or there are complications during delivery.

My weight was a surprise. I didn't look real heavy or pregnant, but when I got on the scale it just jumped right up. I had gained 38 pounds!

Each appointment the nurse would take my heartbeat, blood pressure and see if I had any questions. She explained what was happening with the fetus. She said a baby can hear you when it's seven months along.

Around the end of my pregnancy, the stretch marks came. They're red and look like rips in your skin. You think you can use cocoa butter or a cream from K Mart that says it gets rid of them. Forget it. Nothing works.

The baby was supposed to be born July 14th. It was a week late. I was laying there watching my TV game shows when the contractions started getting hard. I had tears in my eyes.

We all went to the hospital, and when we got there, they said, "You're not going to go for a while."

"Don't tell me that," I said. But then all of a sudden, the contractions were right on top of each other. Contractions are weird. You can't describe them. You think you're going to be prepared for them. You think of the worst pain, and it's worse. It's unbelievable.

But as soon as you see that baby, you forget them.

Rush, Rush, Rush

Misty's five months old now. I never thought it would be this hard. Everything is rush, rush, rush. I don't have any time for myself. And I love my sleep. I get up the first time at four in the morning.

Well, Misty wakes me up and wants to eat. I go to the kitchen, make a bottle, feed her and while I'm burping her, she falls back asleep. A couple of hours later, it's time to get up again.

We shower together. She gurgles the whole time. It's so cute. Then I wash her hair, dress her and put her in a chair while I get myself ready.

By then I have 10 minutes to get us out the door. I make three bottles, get five diapers, some bibs—she's teething. And an extra outfit—sometimes the poop comes out of her Pampers. I put everything in a diaper bag, run it to the car and come back for her. I throw on her snowsuit and hat, pick her up with a big blanket around her face and race her out to the car seat.

I bring her to school with me. There's day care. The pregnant girls and teen mothers help each other. We try to prepare the pregnant ones a little.

I tell them, "You have to do what's best for your baby

and not for you. Sometimes when I'm at my wits' end, my mom will watch her for a half hour so I can just go for a ride. Maybe you can do something like that, too.

Your life is all about your baby. The baby's like your right arm. Whatever you do, your baby's involved. When you're a mother, you have to plan everything. Like, if you can find that baby-sitter, great. If not, you have to sit home. You start getting used to that.

Welfare-to-Work

What's really a surprise, though, is how expensive a child is. I have WIC, a government program where you get some free baby formula, but not enough. You need other food, too. Then there're diapers—$50 a month.

The cheapest little outfit usually costs about 10 bucks. Of course, you need socks, and in the winter you need one-piece T-shirts. For three T-shirts, that's another $10.

Forget the days when welfare meant you could get your own apartment. Now all you hear is "stay with your family." If you get any welfare, there's a time limit. Here in Connecticut, it's two years. They talk about family, finishing school and welfare-to-work.

In our life skills class we talk about budgets. My monthly budget for clothing, food and housing is $2,900. That's the problem. I only make minimum wage, and so does Peter.

After school, I grab all the bottles, put everything in the diaper bag and bring Misty home. My mom watches her from two-thirty to seven o'clock when I work. I don't know how I'd do it without my mother.

Afterwards I come home, feed Misty her cereal, eat supper myself and play with her. I talk to her in weird voices. She looks me right in the eye, curls her little hand around my finger. We connect.

By 10 o'clock she's in bed. We share my room. I used to think it was big. Now it's filled with a changing table, my bed, her crib, my dresser, her dresser and toys.

When I finally stop, that's when I think most about Peter. A month ago, he went down to Texas to try to find better work.

I'm not used to having just myself. I'm used to Peter being around. Our friends say, "You guys are gonna last forever." We'd better! I don't know how single mothers make it.

WELFARE AS WE NO LONGER KNOW IT
Rachel L. Swarns, *The New York Times*, 7/5/98

IN THE 1960s the Federal welfare program was called Aid to Dependent Children. Criticized for discouraging marriage by supporting only single mothers, Federal officials began providing help to couples. While the vast majority of checks continued to flow to single women, the name became Aid to Families with Dependent Children.

Thirty years later, public disapproval of the welfare mother whose children rely on public assistance helped persuade Congress to change the rules and the name again. Temporary Assistance for Needy Families was born. At the state level, Texas created the Workforce Commission to oversee its welfare programs. Michigan dubbed its welfare agency the Family Independence Agency. And Utah started calling its offices "employment centers" and its welfare recipients "job seekers."

"Anyone Can Lie Down and Make Babies."

Jordan, 19 Years Old

Nowadays, lots of young teenagers, 13, 14 years old, want to live in the fast lane. Instead of taking care of business, they want pleasure. Well, partying leads to sex and sex can lead to pregnancy.

I know my lady was 14 when she had my daughter, Zoraida. I was 16. But I couldn't leave them.

That baby is my flesh and blood.

I was scared at first. Zoraida was so small. She'd be laying there, and then she was hungry. But so was I. When you become a father, you learn you have to put your own needs second. Without thinking, you've got to have your kid come first.

Being a good father means you have to be patient.

I want Zoraida to know that even if me and her mother were to have some changes, I'm here to watch her grow. My father wasn't around much when I was young. He still just comes and goes.

His relatives would tell on my mother. Her relatives would tell on my father. He'd go live at his sister's house. She would set him up with women, when she knew he was married to my mother.

Maybe it wasn't my father's fault. I blame him, though. He's supposed to be the man. He's supposed to know that he's got kids around the corner with nothing to eat. When my mother would ask him to help with money and stuff, he'd start a fight.

Not about Sex

This is what I watched growing up. Still, my mother raised me right. I never got in any trouble.

I get on my knees and pray every night. I try to stay around people doing positive things. I pick up the phone and call other young fathers. We keep in touch with one another, keep communicating.

Having a baby made me and my lady responsible. We learned that real life is not about sex. Anyone can lie down and make babies. Life and relationships are more than that. We learned that we've got to show our love and have goals that we're trying to get to.

We said, "We'll stick together and stick it out."

Six weeks ago, we learned another lesson. Sometimes in a relationship, right and wrong come at you at the same time. That doesn't mean you're going to fall down and crumble up. You learn to stay strong.

We lost our sweet two-month-old son. He was a healthy baby, weighed eight pounds and 10 ounces when he was born.

I was at work. I'm an engineer technician. My lady was at home. She woke up and went to check on the baby.

He wasn't breathing.

She gave him mouth-to-mouth to try to save him. Too late. It was a crib death.

We don't blame each other. We just try to be with each other. It's no one's fault. Doctors don't really know why it happens. I told my lady, "God wanted our little boy."

My whole family went to the funeral. I took Zoraida up to see her brother. She thought he was asleep. She's too young to understand. When she gets older, we'll tell her.

As far as my lady, she's going through a depression. She's strong but shy. If she lets out her emotions, she does it on her own.

I keep talking to other fathers. They're really there for me. I let out my pain when I get by myself. I cry.

"Someday I Might Get Married."

Alexsa, 15 Years Old

When I was two, my parents got separated. My mom moved me to Tijuana with her. She says, though, "You missed your dad so much—you were always sick."

We stayed there five years. Finally my mom decided to move back to L.A. with my dad because I couldn't live without him.

Now that I'm grown up, I see that my mom has been miserable because of Dad. She never left again; she would be hurting me. She tells me, "We'd have been much better off without your dad." And that makes me feel guilty. Looking back, I sometimes think she was right.

Too Young to Know

Today I have a child myself. I'm not with my 16-month-old daughter's father. I wasn't happy with him. I thought about my daughter, but I figured she's too young to know the difference between living with both parents or just one.

Although I'm worried about how she'll feel in the future, I don't want to have an emotional relationship with her father. Still, I don't want her to grow up without him.

Something else bothers me, too. Someday I might get married to a different man. How will my daughter feel about that? How will my new husband treat my daughter? Will they be able to get along? I wish I had answers instead of just questions.

SINGLE MOTHERHOOD: STEREOTYPES VS. STATISTICS

Margaret L. Usdansky, *The New York Times*, 2/11/96

THE VAST majority of women having children outside marriage are poor or working class and poorly educated. But they are also diverse: nearly 40 percent are non-Hispanic white and 54 percent are in their 20s.

Studies suggest that young adults increasingly view marriage as an ideal that is beyond their grasp. But contrary to popular opinion, unwed motherhood is often a transitory state. Four out of every 10 mothers whose first birth occurs out of wedlock marry within five years. And some unwed mothers are single only in the legal sense: one in four has a live-in relationship with a man, often, though not always, the child's father, which may encourage marriage later on.

Most young adults say a man who wants to marry should be able to support a family, a standard fewer men without a college degree can meet. Studies find that young women are less likely to marry in places where young employed men are scarce. Marriage is still highly valued, but people don't think it's a realistic possibility.

"I Was a Mad, Stupid Girl Who Wanted to Be Happy."

Written by
Gloria Perez, 18 Years Old
Argo Community High School, Summit, Illinois

I didn't even like him at first. I never thought I'd end up having a baby from him.

We met at a soccer game in our freshman year. He was on the team and I was the manager. The first words he said were, "Give me some water."

"No way," I said, "get it yourself." Then he told me his name, Raymundo, and we just started talking. Gloria-n-Raymundo? That combination didn't sound right to me. By this time in our conversation, I knew he liked me. And I also knew I didn't want him.

He walked me home. I really didn't want him to. I was just being nice. Anyway, his house was before mine. Instead, he kept walking and talking beside me. After that he walked me home every day.

By December four years ago, we'd gone out and broken up and gone out some more. We really didn't fight about anything. I would just find excuses to get rid of him—at least for a while. By the fall, though, we were talking about living together.

Cops Doing the Talking

I was 16. At that moment I was a mad, stupid girl who wanted to be happy and thought that was the way. Me

111

and Ray had plans. Get married, have a nice house, maybe even a dog. All that would start after we both finished college.

My dad met Ray a couple of times, but he only said, "Well, it's your life, Gloria. What can I do about it?" My mom said, "He'll do nothing to help you in the future. Please stay." My grandparents lived with us and they thought we were seeing each other too much. Even then my grandfather would kick Ray out.

My mom told my dad she wanted to call the cops on me. He listened, then said, "Let her go. She'll see how real life is outside." After arguing a few more minutes, my mom went ahead and called them.

I didn't know anything about the laws. My main thought was, "Who's going to call in for me when I don't want to go to school?" My next thought was, "Run! I don't want to be riding in the back of some cop car."

Before I could move, the police got there and told me, "You leave and your mom makes a report—we can go look for you and take you to a jail for teens. You run again and we'll keep bringing you back until we get so sick of it we'll put you in a house for runaways." They didn't scare me.

My mom loves me. I know that now. I just didn't realize that when she had the cops doing the talking.

Sleep in My Own Bed

A week before Thanksgiving, my first Thanksgiving and Christmas without my parents, I started living with Ray and his family. I really missed my mom.

Money was tight. We fought about his family eating the food we bought. We didn't have enough money to wash clothes. Ray did it by hand. His parents would yell at us for staying out late. After a month, I wanted to sleep in my own bed by myself, but I didn't feel I could go back home.

Ray's parents had their own problems, too. His dad would hit his mom and I'd call the cops. Then one day his dad and Raymundo got in such a fight he started pushing our stuff into our car. We had no place to go and, of course, no money.

His mom told his dad, "They go, I'm going, too." So there we were, the three of us. We ended up at his aunt's house for a day or two. Then his dad gave us $300 and his mom had $800 with her. That was enough to rent an apartment together, which was okay, until his mom brought her boyfriend to live with us. Ray didn't like this guy at all.

I Told You So

So that was my life during the year before I became pregnant. Ray couldn't wait for our new life to start with the baby. His mom was happy, even though she didn't say much. His dad only talked when he needed something.

I didn't say anything to my mom about it. She's a proud person. When she makes a decision she sticks with it. It was hard going over to visit. Talking was even harder. In little ways she would say, "I told you so." It hurt to hear that, but she was right. When we were together, she would never cry. I could tell, though, inside, the tears were falling.

One day, when I was about two months pregnant, me and Ray's mom got into an argument. The fight made me nervous and I started to throw up. That scared him and made him mad. Twenty-four hours later we were back living with his dad.

Things got better, but life isn't always a bed of roses. My mom figured out I was pregnant. Still we never mentioned it until I was about seven months. "What kind of life can you give a baby?" she said. "Put it up for adoption."

"It isn't the baby's fault I messed up. My baby moves and I feel it. I can't give it up. Eighteen years from now, I don't want to be out looking for someone who could hate me." My dad just wished us good luck and good health. He loves me, but he always talked better with my half brother.

By the time I was eight months, once again we didn't have the rent money. Ray's dad said he had money in Mexico. "I'll go get it and be back in two weeks," he said.

"He's not coming back, Ray. I can tell," I said once we were alone.

"Think positive. Everything'll be all right."

Three weeks passed. When his dad hadn't returned, I thought, "I just want to die."

Her Rules Again

I swallowed my pride and begged my mom, could we stay with them?

"You can," she said, "but at night Ray sleeps in the car." It was December. Cold out.

"Let him stay inside, please."

"Only if he sneaks past your grandfather."

One day after all this sneaking, I had a long talk with my grandfather. Ray didn't have a job. He was looking, but for some places, of course, you need papers, a driver's license or state ID. He had none of those; he's not a U.S. citizen. Before my grandfather gave his approval, he made me listen to what he had to say.

This wasn't how I wanted it to be. The baby was almost due. We were living with my family. My mom tried to be helpful, but she couldn't handle me, my boyfriend and soon a new baby. She was working two jobs to take care of us, as well as my 15-year-old sister who always wanted name brands. "You left, you 'ho'," my sister would say. "It's not your house anymore."

So Innocent

On January 30th—one more push, and it's a boy! Cesar. The only thing that looks like me is his nose. He has his dad's facial expressions and chubby little cheeks. He looks so innocent. He doesn't know what he's got himself into.

He's not a crybaby. Even when he came out, he only cried for a minute. Now he only cries when he's sleepy or hungry. And since he has no worries, he always wakes up smiling. He makes me laugh. If I turn on the TV to Barney or the Smurfs, he sits there watching like he knows what's going on.

Around midnight, when me and Ray think Cesar is sleeping, we hear something. We turn on the light. There he is, on his back! It's the first time he rolled over. He starts crawling and can play all day. I have to watch everything he gets into.

Now fast forward. Cesar's one year old. Yes, he's the greatest thing that could have happened to me. He's the love of my life. But here's the truth, too. We've gone through so much—Ray losing the job he finally found and having to ask my mom and dad for money for things like milk and diapers.

My mom takes Cesar for a couple hours once in a while. This is progress since she didn't hold him at all the first month. My sister and me get along better. I try to explain life in the outside world, but she's not listening.

I'm a senior. My grades are okay. I hope to become a preschool teacher. I want to go to the community college, where I can drop off Cesar before my classes.

I'm not on welfare or food stamps, but I do have the medical card. As soon as I can get real insurance, I'll be on that. I hope I can teach Cesar to stay away from gangs and drugs the way I have. And I want to talk to him more about sex than my parents did with me.

After three years, me and Ray are still together. Even though we fight once in a while, he's always said he loved me since the beginning. I didn't believe him until things got bad and he was there for me. He wants to get married, but I'm unsure. I love him, but I don't know if that's right for me now. My mom still says we won't last, but I hope we will.

The best advice I can give other teen mothers is to stay in school, and work hard for yourself and your baby.

DADDY DEAREST: DO YOU REALLY MATTER?

Patricia Cohen, *The New York Times*, 7/11/98

MOST unmarried and divorced fathers disappear after the first years of their child's life. Whether rich or poor, married or unmarried, more than 40 percent of men who don't live with their children don't even mention they are fathers in national surveys.

[Studies now being made show] that [college-educated] fathers tend to spend more time with younger children than older ones, more time with boys than girls, more time playing than handling basic needs. Meanwhile, fathers in a lower socioeconomic class tend to spend more time with their children than other fathers do.

[Researchers] of poor, unmarried fathers in Philadelphia are finding that children may do more for fathers than the reverse: without them they might be dead or in jail. Other research hints that children prompt men to get better jobs and work in their communities, and even stay in better health.

"You Ain't Killing My Kid."

Gary,
17 Years Old

118

120

120

Doris Stiles-Glazer, Psychologist
Family Therapist and Teacher of Parenting Classes,
Coral Gables, Florida

Your model for how you parent comes from your home. Unless you've hung around with other families and seen something different, what you're going to do with your own children is repeat what happened to you.

A good way to get more information on how to raise children is to take a course at a local high school. You can also talk to other parents, check for help at clinics and read books on the topic.

It's up to you to evaluate that information when it comes to your own baby. You want to make the best decisions to meet your baby's needs. And this includes understanding child development—how children change as they get older.

Let's look at some examples. Making sure that your children are safe includes taking them for medical examinations and getting them inoculations. It also includes things such as knowing that babies can't see danger. Never assume that even a two- or three-year-old can be left alone.

The parent's job is to provide safe limits. When children are too little to understand a dangerous situation, remove them from it. Put them in a playpen, or remove the dangerous object and replace it with a safe object.

When children are a bit older and they're doing something you don't want them to do, use a distraction. Focus their attention on something else.

You can put them behind a gate across the door of a room. You don't want to put them behind a solid, shut door. Children feel frightened by that. The object is not to scare your kids, but to set reasonable limits.

Time-Out

When children are about two, if they do something you don't like, you can start using what we call "time-out." Time-out is putting children in a place where they can still see you, but they have to sit for a brief period of time. The older the child, the longer the time-out. For a two-year-old, about a minute is plenty.

What you're trying to do is teach your children self-control and self-discipline. And you're trying to do this without hitting them. I'm for discipline, but real discipline doesn't involve hitting a child. Once you start hitting, they're going to expect to be hit.

Parenting is a tough job. It can be frustrating. People respond to that frustration in different ways. Most people say, "If I'm frustrated, I try to take time-out from the situation until I can collect myself. I try to exercise. I try to do things for myself away from the house. I try to seek information on how to solve my parenting problems."

But some people say, "I can't stand it anymore." They respond to that frustration by becoming withdrawn and depressed. When that happens, you neglect your children.

Big Warning Sign

There are warning signs that you may be neglecting your children. Your children complain a lot about physical problems. They have accidents. They don't sleep well. They look sad and withdrawn.

Sometimes people who have had abusive parents try to do the opposite of the family patterns. Because you don't want to repeat the abuse, you become neglectful parents. You don't know what else to do. If others are telling you that something's wrong with your children, that's a big warning sign of neglect. Listen to them and get help.

Some people respond to that frustration with aggression, and then you get physical abuse. You don't always know you're physically abusive to your children. You just think you're disciplining them. You say you beat them to teach them not to beat somebody else. You're trying to make them be good people.

Warning signs of physical abuse would be that you scream at your children. You shake them. You hit them. You leave them unattended when they are in danger. If you recognize these signs, you should get help.

Completely Inappropriate

With sexual abuse, you're dealing with something different. Sexual abuse is interacting with a child in a way that stimulates or arouses you or the child. It's completely inappropriate. It's usually an addictive behavior on the part of the person who's doing it. And it's repetitive. If you do it once, you're going to do it again.

People who are sexually abusive to children know they are. If you are a survivor of sexual abuse, without exception, you ought to talk to somebody about that. The biggest setup for somebody to become abusive is to have been abused and to have not resolved it. That goes for men and women.

Nobody is going to love your children more than you. And your children, when they're babies, need you to be at their side at all times. Until they can do for themselves, you're their eyes, their ears, their hands. Your children become the best people they can be—with your guidance.

"I'm There for My Kids."

Anthony, 22 Years Old

Oh, man, am I a father! There are three different mothers, three different kids, and one me. But I deal with it.

Along the way I've learned some stuff that, maybe, can help you, too. Let's deal first with when girls are pregnant. Some of them feel they're carrying all the burden. They get into moods. You're always hearing, "I'm fat. I'm ugly. I'm this. I'm that."

The pressure gets so much it's, like, pushing you away. That's when a lot of you begin to be sorry. You want to just lay the girls, make them pregnant and run out the door. I say, "Be a man. Stick it out." You've got to handle the frustration of their taking out their feelings on you.

Tell them, "I'm there for you, and that child." At times, though, it's never enough. They treat you like a worm inside a barrel of apples.

I've been there to see one of my babies born in the house. We couldn't make it to the hospital. The paramedic happened to be a reverend, too. He blessed my baby boy right there in the bedroom.

I've seen my two other babies, two girls, born in the hospitals. Whatever way it happens, I'm telling you, it is a shocker.

With one, the mother barely got through the emergency room doors and the baby came out. But with the very first one, I felt like the mother, Lisa, and I went through the whole thing—together.

I went to the washup outside the delivery room. I put on the blue surgical suit just like the doctors. They said she was going to have a C-section, a cesarean section. I could go behind the glass and see all they were doing, blood and everything.

They had her stretched out with her arms locked to the sides of the operating table. They had these machines and monitors on Lisa. I watched them open her up. I saw the birth. I saw this funny-looking, snakelike thing, the umbilical cord. I saw the afterbirth. When you see the baby, you can see right through, see the veins. I wondered, "How does the baby survive all that?" I got weak in the stomach. I fainted.

When I came to, I was lying in the bed next to Lisa in the recovery room. She'd gone through the operation, was cut open, sewed up and wheeled back out.

Kids Get Sick

At 15, I was a first-time father of a baby girl. Me and Lisa named her Dorian. I was so excited, I overheated. Everything, I figured, would be roses.

Another thing I learned is, good or bad, when you're a parent and it comes to your children, you've got to deal with it. Even if you're a perfect parent, kids get sick and hurt: asthma attacks, fevers, cuts, allergies, sore throats.

Once one of my kids was sick and we didn't know what was wrong. The mother, Kelly, said, "Maybe he has a cold or something. He's been in the house for two days."

We talked it over, and then we had to decide what to do. Finally I said, "He's going to the hospital."

So I'm coming in the hospital door and I'm in my T-shirt with my jacket wrapped around him. I walk straight into the emergency room. I don't even register. They start hassling me about documents for the baby. I keep saying, "But I'm his father. The mother is at her mother's house in Brooklyn with the papers."

The doctors are looking at me, looking at the baby. I hear one say something about child abuse. They want to call the police and I'm just trying to help my kid.

See, I didn't know until later that the baby had a 105.9° temperature, pneumonia and two ear infections. At the time, I didn't know it was such an emergency.

Interference

My parents are married for 27 years. I'm not doing that well, and sometimes I think it comes down to interference.

Maybe Lisa would have been my only girlfriend or wife if I'd put my foot down and said, "Listen. We can't afford this and that. Let's just be ourselves."

But Lisa's into her mother and her sisters. She was raised without her father. And because he was not there, she tends to shy away from men.

We started arguing. My parents let me run my life, but they do give advice. My parents say, "In any relationship, no matter how extreme the problem is, give yourself time. Put it aside. Go back to it. Talk about it. Work on it."

All I heard from Lisa was "A man's supposed to do this. A man's supposed to do that." I was living at home, working for my father. I was still in school. I was seeing her and Dorian every day.

I felt I was accomplishing. I also felt I was being used. And anytime a male feels that way, he's going to back up. "Enough is enough," I said to myself.

But then, I had to figure out how to keep seeing my baby, Dorian, with me and Lisa over. I knew it wasn't the materialistic things you give your children. It's the quality time you spend with them.

How could I talk to my child, play with her, share things that I'd like her to know? Lisa told me she had other plans. She wanted to take my daughter and go on about her business. I felt terrible. I wanted to be there for Dorian. "Okay," I said, "you want to be in your world. I want to be in my world. But Dorian has still got to be in the middle."

Mommy against Daddy

After Lisa, I got involved with Kelly. She already had a son before she had ours. I told her, "I'm with you now. You've got my kid. I'll try to take care of the whole thing."

I felt good knowing that I could go out every day, work and put food on the table. I didn't have to turn to my mother and father. It was all me. I was doing things for my son.

With him and my daughter, I started learning more about kids' tricks. Kids like to play Mommy against Daddy and Daddy against Mommy. Meanwhile, Mommy and Daddy are standing there, looking at each other, saying, "Why did you do that? Why didn't you tell me first?"

What I try to do is this. Say Dorian tells me, "Daddy, I want to go to the movies."

I ask her, "What does your mother say about that?"

"Oh, Mommy says it's okay," she says.

Then I tell her, "Sweetheart, I'm not saying no, I'm saying maybe. First let me double-check with your mother. If she says all right, we'll go."

What you learn is kids lie. Her mother had already told Dorian "no way" to the movies. If I didn't check first, if I went and got the tickets, Lisa and I would have been in another fight.

My advice is you and the children's mother should talk to each other before taking any action. I don't care if it's a single parent or both parents under the same roof, you have to keep communicating. And that link cannot be broken when it comes to your children.

Sure, it's tough to deal with not being there in your kids' life every day. When you are around, you have to be careful not to cause too much confusion or any misunderstanding between you and your children.

You have to keep letting them know that you love them. You want them to be with you anytime they're willing. They're always welcome. At the same time, you don't want to press yourself on them.

To me, it's like a chess game. One person has to move before the other one. And when that one person—your child—moves, you take the same step. You have to take your arguments with the mother and put them aside. Children need two parents to feed and clothe them. So any arguments between you two are not important to them.

A Backbone Man

So I've got Dorian on my mind and my little boy on my mind. And one day I'm coming home from work and I find Kelly in bed with her ex-boyfriend—with my son there.

I lost my mind. I broke up stuff. The police came and

at first arrested me for disorderly conduct. Lisa used that as an excuse to say I couldn't see Dorian, but I'd better keep sending a monthly support check. If I didn't, she'd take me to court.

I decided Kelly wasn't any better than Lisa. I moved out.

When I was 20, my grandfather died. He was a deep down man, a backbone man. Whatever he did with work, first he made sure everybody at his home was all right. I decided I wanted to be that way, too.

I made a commitment to Lucy. We had a baby, a daughter, Tracy.

My favorite thing is to get all my kids together. The other day, my two oldest started climbing on me, play-wrestling. I played until my back got stiff. I tell them they're sisters and brothers. Saying they're half only confuses them.

As your kids grow up, you've got to confront them. If you want them to have sense, talk to them like adults. My one-year-old, Tracy, can sit in front of the TV and remember a song off a commercial. That tells me she's ready to hear some about life and reality. Lucy found a young fathers' program for me. I was ready to go. I opened up as soon as I started.

I only wondered why there aren't more programs. The ladies have their educational classes, their parenting classes. What young fathers have are people telling us, "You're not going to make it." That makes the young fathers I know fight even more to do better.

We all need help to make ourselves good role models for our kids. I've learned that a man can help make a baby, and a woman can have a baby. But a man and a woman can take care of children equally well.

TEEN SEX AND PREGNANCY

Facts in Brief, The Alan Guttmacher Institute, 7/96

THIRTEEN PERCENT of all U.S. births are to teens. Eighty-five percent of teen pregnancies are unplanned, accounting for about 1/4 of all accidental pregnancies yearly. Twenty-five percent of teenage mothers have a second child within two years of their first.

CONTRARY MESSAGE ON TEENAGE PREGNANCY

Richard T. Cooper, *The Los Angeles Times*, 5/24/97

TEENAGERS do not have problems because they have babies; they have babies because they have problems. Child-bearing is a symptom, not a cause. Instead of crusading against the symptoms, society should be working on the underlying causes—such things as poverty, dysfunctional families, physical and sexual abuse of young girls, poor school performance and behavioral problems.

"I'm Beating the Odds."

Yveline, 21 Years Old

I didn't know I was pregnant. I kept having my period. Normally I would have it for five days. That May, the year my sister got her first communion, I only bled for two days.

I thought, "As long as I'm bleeding, I'm fine."

Anyway, my mother had once told me, "Babies are dropped from the sky and fall into your stomach. After you get married, you're ready to have a baby. God decides when."

I wasn't married. I couldn't get pregnant. But I was, and I was only 11.

Poking at My Body

One morning I came out of the shower and my mom said, "What's that?!" I had a line from my belly button to my breasts. Next thing I knew, it was, "Put on your clothes. You're going to the doctor!"

There were five doctors in the hospital room. They kept poking at my body until it hurt. One doctor said, "I'm sure it didn't hurt when you opened your legs."

Another doctor, a lady, took me in her office and started showing me books about people giving birth. "Do you know about this?" she asked me.

I didn't.

She told me what abortion was. What adoption was. What having a baby was like.

After I left her office, she asked my mother to go in. They were together for maybe five minutes. When my mother came out, I could see smoke pouring out of her ears. She slapped me and said, "We're going home."

"You need to return tomorrow," the doctor said as we walked to the elevator.

We went back for the results of the urine and blood tests. I was almost five months pregnant. "What do you want to do?" the doctor asked my mother.

"I want her to have an abortion."

"We can't do it. It would be risky. Your daughter's too young and too many weeks pregnant. She waited too long."

"I don't care!" my mother screamed. "Nothing's going to happen to her. She'll be fine."

The doctor refused.

See, my mother was ill at that time. She was going to the hospital a lot. I think it was even causing some mental problems. At that time, she lost her job, lost the house to the bank, lost everything.

Crybaby

The next thing I knew, a social worker came to the house. They took me and my sister to family court. The judge asked, "Did I want to go home?"

"No," I said, "I'm scared of my mother." She was very upset with me. I thought she might beat me.

The court sent me to a shelter for unwed mothers. Of the 12 of us there, I was the youngest. The other girls called me Crybaby. I was depressed about everything.

I didn't like the changes in my body. I felt heavy, fat, like I couldn't move. We had mandatory exercise classes. Lamaze-method childbirth classes. Breathing classes. I was told if I didn't do them, giving birth would be painful. Sometimes, though, I wasn't in the mood.

We had chores to do, too. We took turns cooking. The food was delicious. After that first month, things got better. One of the workers would stick up for me. I could come to her office and talk whenever I wanted.

There was a regular school just for us. We'd go every day. I wanted to keep up in those classes. I always had ambition. I was in seventh grade.

I was strongly thinking about adoption. The social workers were pushing it. They didn't come out and say, "We think you should give up your child." But I could tell that's what they thought. I was getting scared of childbirth. I heard women talk about Eve in the Bible and how this was punishment from God. "Labor is the most painful thing that can happen to a woman," they'd say.

I never heard anyone say raising a child is more difficult and painful than having a baby.

Secret Life

I was 12 when I had my daughter. I named her Katherine. At first, I didn't want to see her. I was going to give her up for adoption. Then I told the social worker, "I need more time."

They made arrangements for me and Katherine to go into foster care. The problem was they couldn't find anyone who would take us together. She went one place; I went another.

Where I went there were other foster kids, an adopted one, and even grandchildren all in this one home. My first month I didn't talk to anyone. I turned on the soaps, lay around and ate.

The second month I started talking, especially to JayJay, a foster child who was now grown up. He told me, "People are going to put papers in front of you to sign away your child. Take time to think or you'll regret it."

The social worker kept coming by. Sometimes I didn't even know what she was talking about. I was in another world. She wanted me to go into therapy. I said, "School will be my therapy."

In March, I went back to seventh grade. There were only a couple of people that knew I was a mother. That was okay. I always thought everybody had a secret life. This was mine.

One Saturday my foster nephew said there was a man at the door. It was my father. I hadn't spoken to him since I had my daughter. I was scared and happy and confused to see him. Once I told him what was going on, he said, "Of course, I don't hate you."

That same day, I called the social worker and told her, "Throw the adoption papers away. I'm keeping my daughter." I still cry with happiness when I think about that decision.

The social worker started telling me about shelters they had for teenage mothers and their children. The problem was I was 13, and back then you had to be 14 to get in. Plus they had to have room.

When Katherine was almost a year old, I began to visit her every weekend. I had no idea how to be a mother. I hadn't seen her the whole time. All I had was her picture to carry in my wallet.

The day before my 14th birthday, Katherine and I were reunited. We moved into the New York Foundling Mother and Child Program in the Bronx. It was like a house where there were mothers, their children and a housemother.

The others had been with their children since giving birth. I didn't even know what to say to Katherine. And she was really quiet. I didn't blame her. She was two. She went from her foster home straight to me.

Finally, I said, "I have to start being a mother. I'll figure out how the system works and take advantage of everything that's available to teenage moms."

Learn from Other People

You can learn from other people. To do that you build a network. This network is made up of other teenage parents. You want to know what they've found out. What help are they getting? Do they go to parenting classes? Do they have free medical care? Do they know where to buy discount kids' clothes? Whatever. And the next question is, Where did they go to get that help?

Then you decide what you need and go do the same.

You also want to build relationships with some trusted adults—social workers, a therapist, somebody like that. Why? Because they know things. If you show them you mean business, they'll help. But you can't just say, "Please, help me," and sit back and wait. You have to be optimistic and figure out what you want.

Maybe these adults don't have all the information you want right away, but they know how to get it. And if they don't know, they can find out.

For example, one time I found out that my school had a work-study program: work one week, school one week. I wanted to know how to get in to that program, and if I did get in, could I save everything I earned? I wanted that money to go toward an apartment, and I wanted to find a cheap apartment as soon as possible.

In Three Years

See, I had this image of where I wanted to be in three years. I needed to find out, How do I get there? What does the city have to offer to help me get there? What is available to me before I turn 18? What is available after that?

Cassandra, a social worker, helped me a lot. I was lucky. Sometimes, though, the first person you ask won't pay much attention. Go to a second person or a third.

You have to do your own footwork, too. Double-check what they tell you. Sure, you get frustrated. But there's always someone who'll help you. By getting help, you end up helping your child. That's what this is about: being a good parent.

You have to make your children your priority. You have to be willing to sacrifice for them without being all droopy.

I'm not going to lie to you. I was not a totally boring teenager. I still went out. I still had sex. But, at the same time, I graduated from high school with flying colors. After four years at the Foundling, I finally moved into my own apartment in public housing.

Katherine was six and I had just turned 18. I knew I was starting college that fall. It would be hard. So that summer I was wild. Mind you, I still took care of business. My rule was, unless I was confident my daughter was fine, I wouldn't party.

I worked full-time Monday through Friday 8:30 A.M. to 4:30 P.M. But every Friday night, Saturday night and Sunday night that summer I went out. I went to clubs. I loved reggae music. I liked to talk to guys with nice cars. Come Monday, I was a zombie.

And then it was September. I became a college student.

I'm 21 now and a senior at Hunter College in New York City. I'm in a scholarship program. I have two part-time jobs, one at Citibank Tax Shelter and the other at Payne-Whitney Psychiatric Center. I plan to go to graduate school and, maybe, do research about AIDS among teenagers.

Katherine and I have a great relationship—more like sisters. I tell her, "Sure, we have a wonderful life together. But motherhood is hard." Where we live, we see moms on drugs using their babies to beg for money. Katherine and I talk about things like that, too.

Such a Challenge

I remind her, I never got pregnant a second time. There was no man, no love strong enough to make me have another child as a teenager.

I even tell her there are moments when I wonder what my life would have been like if I hadn't had her. "It's not like I regret having you," I say. "It's just that I never was a teenager. It must be fun." But my Katherine is my life. I love watching her grow up.

I felt such satisfaction when she took her first step. I was so proud when she brought home her first 100 from school.

I thought, "Hey, I'm doing this right. I'm beating the odds against teen mothers." I put a lot into being a good parent, but what I'm getting back is even greater. It keeps me moving. It's such a challenge.

I'm mushy with my daughter. I hug her a lot. I love to tell her I love her. I just feel all her love in return. There's nothing else in the world quite like it, the love between a mother and child.

PART VII

KIDS

TALKING ABOUT

THE END OF THIS BOOK
AND THE BEGINNING OF
YOUR NEXT STEP

"Statistics Are Not the Only Predictors of the Future"

On these pages you read other teenagers' stories. For those working on a research paper, I hope you found the information beneficial.

For those involved in a pregnancy or parenting, I'm glad you took this step toward making life decisions. Each of you writes your own story. You may have an uphill battle, but remember, statistics are not the only predictors of the future. You are special and unique. Keep making the choice to involve as many wise and trusted people, and as many good resources as possible, in helping you.

Below is a list of toll-free telephone numbers related to these issues. In some cases, you'll first hear a machine. In other cases, you'll hear a series of commands about pushing number one for details about employment, pushing two for details about education, and so on.

Be patient. That's part of life, too.

Childhelp
  USA's National Child Abuse Hotline   800-422-4453

GED Hotline   800-626-9433

Growing Up Healthy Hotline   800-522-5006

National Abortion Federation   800-772-9100

National AIDS Hotline   800-342-2473

National AIDS Hotline (Spanish)   800-344-7432

National Child Welfare Resource Center   800-435-7543

National Clearinghouse on Family
  Support & Children's Mental Health   800-628-1696

National Drug & Alcohol
  Treatment Referral Routing Service   800-662-4357

National Life Center Hotline/
  Pregnancy Hotline   800-848-5683

National Sexually Transmitted
  Diseases Hotline   800-232-2579

National Welfare-to-Work Institute   800-232-2579

National Youth Crisis Hotline   800-448-4663

Twenty Years of Change

To Media Specialists,
Teachers and Other Interested Adults

I remember in the summer of 1978 going to the first-ever teen conference on sex and pregnancy among adolescents. It was held in Atlanta and 3,500 kids showed up along with adults involved in the issue.

"Sex is natural to being human and part of being born human," an adult speaker said to the audience. "There's another part, though—your mind. You must make choices.

"Ask yourself, 'What kind of a sexual person do I want to be? How will I know I'm ready to accept the responsibility of actual physical, sexual intercourse?'

"Decisions about sex are no different from any other important life decisions. They demand your best thinking and your highest morality."

Those words were applauded, but the fact remained: Sex is often initiated on a hormonal impulse. The result?

One million mainly unmarried teenagers became pregnant that year and the next and the next. Today, the hard numbers are about the same.

Parents' Advice

Then and now teen females are romantics. They want to be swept up in the arms of Prince Charming, get married and have a family. More than half of them plan on working outside the home, too.

Then and now, the majority of teens, male and female, say they value their parents' advice. They remind me that adolescence may be years of separation "but not, like, total abandonment," as one girl put it. They want to be close to their families. They want specific advice on the opposite sex, dating, sexually transmitted diseases and how to say no.

When those conversations take place, the teen offspring are more likely to value their virginity, have fewer partners in general and use contraceptives. When those conversations don't occur, kids turn to each other and/or their schools to fill the void. And according to the Sexuality Information and Education Council of the United States (SEICUS) fewer than 10 percent of American students receive a comprehensive sex education.

Just-the-Facts/Just-Say-No

Six hundred and seventeen high schools now have school-based clinics. Twenty years ago there were only a handful. However, in many schools the clinics provide little education and are not allowed to give out any form of birth control, condoms included.

Meanwhile, the number of family planning clinics has gone down. And it still takes a confidant, together kid to call a clinic, make an appointment and show up. If they call saying they're pregnant, they receive attention. If they're asking about birth control information, the attention is limited.

Twenty years ago HIV-AIDS had not been identified. Now I meet young people who have seen friends and family members living with it and dying from it. For this reason, among others, there's an increased condom use for many in the current sexually active adolescent population.

In fact, contraceptive use is way up. I came across a study that said only 11 percent of teens used condoms in 1980. Now it's 44 percent. And city teenagers are increasingly turning to the effective Depo-Provera injections or Norplant.

Other adolescents are simply choosing not to have sex. The just-the-facts philosophy meets the just-say-no approach. From what I hear, today among some teens it's okay and even cool to be a self-proclaimed virgin. Students frequently tell me they want books written on abstinence to support the choice they're making.

Teenagers have been influenced by the pro-choice /pro-life battle. They wrestle more with their consciences than they did before. Although I recorded stories in the past where teenagers talked of dodging yelling demonstrators at abortion providers, the level of violence and media attention has escalated over the intervening years.

Because of changes in the laws restricting abortion and a decrease of providers, it is harder for adolescents to have this procedure than in the past. Simultaneously, though, I find the number of theoretical pro-life teens has increased. However, similar to women of all ages, when it turns into a real-life decision, young adults have been known to change their minds.

Recently with adoption, birth fathers have gained more rights, as have a few highly publicized birth mothers in reclaiming their children. And foreign adoptions especially from Korea, China and Eastern Europe have increased. Foster care remains an often troubling and troubled solution to a whole series of human problems.

A Childhood Taken Away

Because I also have written on sexual abuse and sexual assault, over the years I kept hearing about older boyfriends, false promises, pressured sex, sexual abuse at home. Today studies reveal that these male partners weren't teens themselves. They were men 20 and older impregnating girls. Also girls who have been sexually abused are more likely to be sexually active and have children at younger ages.

In *Kids Having Kids* I wondered in print, Does the pregnancy cause the problems or the problems cause the pregnancy? And does the same cause and effect hold true with parenting? Today that is how the discussion is frequently framed.

Then as now, a childhood is taken away when a youngster becomes a parent. They have so many problems going into it, those who overcome this incredible challenge should receive much deserved praise. And praise should go to their families, too. Regardless of age, parenting is not a solo operation. The ones I see who often soar are those with the best network of emotional and practical support.

The number of programs, organizations and outreach aimed at teen mothers has increased over the years. What I've never understood, however, is why fathers—teen and older—have been so overlooked. There's almost no scientific data to back up why and how dads actually matter. And unless we can accurately ascertain that information, how can we try to fill the gap when he isn't there?

It's taken until the 21st century for researchers to study and map the role of the father in today's family.

One in Three Children

At present one in four children six and under is growing up in poverty. I fear that because the role of the federal government has been reduced in terms of financial assistance to the children from impoverished families, we could soon be looking at one in three.

For better or worse, the safety net has been pulled from under many young moms. Do teenagers now say to themselves, I can't afford to have unprotected sex and risk the possibility of an unplanned pregnancy? I won't become a parent until I am financially secure? My instincts tell me that's not the case.

Success Stories

I have never learned officially that one of my books has been censored or banned. It's always after the fact. I'll come across something on the Internet, a friend will send me a newspaper clip, a librarian will mention in passing she was told not to shelve that particular title. Equally upsetting, a publisher will explain that certain salespeople won't handle books on some of the topics I cover.

If this ever happens in your area, please let me know. I'd welcome the opportunity to meet with members of your student body and/or the community to discuss why this has taken place.

I'm proud of the work I do. The letters from readers let me know in vivid and moving detail how vital it is. The stories, they tell me, touch their lives, help them over-come their sense of isolation and offer them a starting point from which to look for solutions. I also hear from kids for whom parenting has turned their lives around, focusing them, giving them a greater purpose to achieve.

Last summer it made my day to meet a 21-year-old man whose then-teen mom had let me interview her for the original *Kids Having Kids*. The two of them together make up one of the many stories that start out on the pages of my books as problems to overcome and end up as remarkable successes.

For those who have bought this book and encouraged teachers to use it in their classrooms, I thank you. For those who've placed it in the hands of your students, I thank you. And for those who've had to defend that choice, I thank you again. My work would exist in a vacuum if not for you. May we continue to help each other and the teenagers in our lives. They are our future.

Kay Franey, Life Skills Teacher
Severn School, Severna Park, Maryland

I put on a tape of a colicky, crying baby and say to the students, "Write a letter to your parents telling them you're pregnant or you've gotten a girl pregnant."

Sometimes I hear, "Turn off that terrible tape!" Other times I hear, "Girls at this school don't get pregnant." It's the fantasy under which they operate. In reality, in our community, abortion is often the option of choice.

But soon one student, then another will start talking about personal life experiences: a friend from middle school who had a baby at 16; another who opted for adoption. The class discussions go from there.

As the teacher, I don't give my opinion. Instead I tell them that in our culture their generation is bombarded with sexual messages—minus the consequences. This is a tremendous disservice to them. They are part of our world and should have conversations about causes and effects. I'm there to answer questions and offer information.

While doing that, I try to cover what I see as the five dimensions of their lives: mental, spiritual, physical, emotional and social.

Options and Consequences

In presenting pregnancy, I get the conversations going with these kinds of questions:

- If you choose to be abstinent, who would support you?
- If you choose to be sexually active, what are some over the-counter and prescription birth control products?
- What does each cost?
- What impact do you think alcohol and drugs have on the use of birth control?
- Why do some teenagers choose not to use birth control?
- What are sexually transmitted diseases (STDs) and what are the chances of contracting them?
- What is the relationship between STDs and infertility?
- What do you know about HIV-AIDS?
- If there's a pregnancy, what are your options?
- What are the (mental, spiritual, physical, emotional, social) consequences of each option for you and your family?
- What medical attention does each option involve?
- What are the financial ramifications?
- What do you see as your financial responsibility?
- What are the laws?

Of course, this is not a one-time discussion. Ideally it should be part of the student's scheduled, ongoing classes.

MORE READING

Unless noted, these are young adult books.

Arthur, Shirley. *Surviving Teen Pregnancy: Your Choices, Dreams, and Decisions,* revised edition. Buena Park, CA: Morning Glory Press, 1996.

Ayer, Eleanor H. *Everything You Need to Know about Teen Fatherhood,* revised edition. New York: Rosen Publishing Group, 1995.

Berlfein, Judy. *Teen Pregnancy.* San Diego, CA: Lucent Books, 1992.

Gartner, Richard. *Sexual Betrayal of Boys: Aftermath and Treatment as Men.* New York: Guilford Press, forthcoming. (Adult)

Gravelle, Karen, and Leslie Peterson. *Teenage Fathers.* Englewood Cliffs, NJ: J. Messner, 1992.

Jakobson, Cathryn. *Think about Teen Pregnancy.* New York: Walker, 1993.

Jamiolkowski, Raymond M. *A Baby Doesn't Make the Man: Alternative Sources of Power and Manhood for Young Men.* New York: Rosen Publishing Group, 1997.

Lang, Paul C., and Susan S. Lang. *Teen Fathers*. New York: Franklin Watts, 1995.

Lindsay, Jeanne Warren, and Jean Brunelli. *Your Pregnancy and Newborn Journey: How to Take Care of Yourself and Your Newborn If You're a Pregnant Teen*. Buena Park, CA: Morning Glory Press, 1994.

Luker, Kristin. *Dubious Conceptions: The Politics of Teenage Pregnancy*. Cambridge, MA: Harvard University Press, 1996. (Adult)

Mucciolo, Gary. *Everything You Need to Know about Birth Control*. New York: Rosen Publishing Group, 1996.

Orenstein, Peggy. *School Girls. Young Women, Self-Esteem, and the Confidence Gap*. New York: Doubleday, 1994. (Adult)

WITH THANKS

Many thanks to my extended family and support team: My partner, Stan Mack; my sisters, Barbara and Carolyn; and the rest, Kenny, Peter, Stephanie, Kerri, Frieda and Ernie; as well as Joanne Althoff, Phyllis Cadle, Lucy Cefalu, Bridget Funk, Jane Goldberg, Ted and Harriet Gottfried, Carole Mayedo, Rosemarie and Marvin Mazor, Betty Medsger, Mike Sexton, Deborah Udin and the now (widely) dispersed Third Thursday Group, including Mary Kay Blakely, Andrea Boroff Eagan, Kathryn Kilgore, and Jane O'Reilly.

Linda Johnson, Counselor, Sam Yeto High School, Fairfield, CA, encouraged students to contribute essays for this edition. Joy McKay, Language Arts Teacher, Argo Community High School, Summit, IL, worked with her students to write and rewrite their life stories for use in this book. Thanks to those remarkable teenagers and to you adults for your help and long distance encouragement for my projects.

Invaluable assistance was also provided by the following people: Kathy Ebel, Lisa Stump and my editor, E. Russell Primm; plus Gail Barraco, Media Specialist, Groton Middle/High School, Groton, NY; Marianne Gregory, Art Teacher, and Ed Markarian, Language Arts Teacher, Franklin High School, Los Angeles, CA; Dixie Hewitt, Media Specialist, San Saba High School, San Saba, TX; Kathleen O'Donnel, NYPL-CLASP, and

Larry Williams, Media Specialist, Public Library-Inwood, NY; Ellen Rubin, Media Specialist, Wallkill Senior High School, Wallkill, NY; Bonnie Wojnowski, Media Specialist, Candor Middle/High School, Candor, NY.

These sources were of great help on the 1992 edition:
Andrea Rose Askowitz and Veena Cabreros-Sud, SOS, NY, NY; Maria Delgado, Marie Jean, and Yoli Rojas, NYC Department of Health, Bureau of School Children and Adolescent Health, City Volunteer Corps, NY, NY; Martha Kuss, Media Specialist, Crawford High School, San Diego, CA; Amy Miller, M.D., Director, Chemically Abusing Problem Adolescence Program, Trinity House of St. Luke's-Roosevelt Hospital, NY, NY; Lynn Paltrow, American Civil Liberties Union/Reproductive Freedom Project, NY, NY; Tamar Raphael, Feminist Majority, Arlington, VA; Ellen Ramsay, Media Specialist, Amphitheater High School, Tucson, AZ; Susan Tew, The Alan Guttmacher Institute, NY, NY; Cynthia Wilson, Office of Adolescent Parenting Program, LYFE, NY, NY.

And thank you to the teenagers who shared their stories. This book wouldn't have been possible without you.

INDEX

Spence-Chapin (adoption
 agency), 64
STDS, 27, 32–33
Stretch marks, 103
Suicide, 24
Support networks, 136, 145
Syphilis, 27, 32–33

Teen fathers, 47, 65–66
Teen mothers, 102–107
Teen pregnancy, 6–12,
 38, 131
 decline in rates of, 38
Telephone numbers to
 call, 141
Temporary Assistance for
 Needy Families, 106
"Time out," 122–123
Toll-free telephone
 numbers, 141
Toxemia, 36
Trimesters, 31

Ultrasound test, 54
Under-reporting, of
 sexual activity, 17
United States, birth rates
 in, 38
Urination, frequency of,
 32

Virginity, 6–19, 144
 reclaiming of, 8–9
Welfare, 105–106

Welfare-to-work, 105–106
WIC program, 105
Workforce Commission,
 106
Work-study programs,
 136

Young fathers groups,
 38–39, 109, 130

Who's Who

Janet Bode's titles, including *Beating the Odds, Voices of Rape,* and *Heartbreak and Roses,* have received numerous best-book awards from such groups as the American Library Association, the International Reading Association and the National Council for Social Studies. *Different Worlds: Interracial and Cross-Cultural Dating,* which inspired a CBS-TV Schoolbreak Special, was a finalist for the NAACP Humanitas Award and a nominee for four daytime Emmies. *The Oprah Winfrey Show, Larry King Live* and *20/20* are just a few of the programs on which Bode has appeared to discuss today's issues.

Reporter/cartoonist **Stan Mack** has written and illustrated more than 15 children's books, contributed regularly to such publications as *The New York Times, Natural History Magazine* and *Print,* and created weekly strips for the *Village Voice* and *Adweek* magazine. His latest book-length titles are: *Stan Mack's Real Life American Revolution* and *The Story of the Jews: A 4,000 Year Adventure.*

Ida Marx Blue Spruce is a cartoonist/illustrator whose work has appeared in a variety of publications, among them *The New Yorker, The New Asian Times, Fantagraphics* and the books *Mind Riot: Coming of Age in Comix* and *Voices of Rape* (revised edition).